THE SCHOLARLY WORKFLOW IN THE DIGITAL AGE

Charleston Briefings: Trending Topics for Information Professionals is a thought-provoking series of brief books concerning innovation in the sphere of libraries, publishing, and technology in scholarly communication. The briefings, growing out of the vital conversations characteristic of the Charleston Conference and *Against the Grain*, will offer valuable insights into the trends shaping our professional lives and the institutions in which we work.

The *Charleston Briefings* are written by authorities who provide an effective, readable overview of their topics—not an academic monograph. The intended audience is busy nonspecialist readers who want to be informed concerning important issues in our industry in an accessible and timely manner.

Matthew Ismail, Editor in Chief

THE SCHOLARLY WORKFLOW IN THE DIGITAL AGE

STEVEN WEILAND

Published in the United States of America by
ATG LLC (Media)
Manufactured in the United States of America

DOI: https://doi.org/10.3998/mpub.12119260

ISBN 978-1-941269-44-2 (paper)
ISBN 978-1-941269-45-9 (ebook)
ISBN 978-1-941269-46-6 (open access)

http://against-the-grain.com

CONTENTS

INTRODUCTION

The workflow names what is done in the conduct of research reflecting its individual, institutional, technological, and social conditions. It displays the conventions that produce knowledge across the disciplines and the innovations that enhance and challenge scholarly and scientific routines. The workflow registers the impact of libraries and publishing, and their increasingly digital operations, on academic work. Attention to the workflow shows how the conditions of research can be improved, productivity strengthened, and satisfaction in scholarly and scientific careers sustained.

"Workflow" came into English about one hundred years ago to name the deliberate or rational organization of labor often associated with manufacturing systems and the assembly line. Indeed, in the "Taylorism" of industrializing America, the workflow became a location for making standardization and efficiency the essence of work. But no one would mistake a biology laboratory or a historian's study as sites of carefully calibrated time-controlled actions. There are planning and structure, and a recognizable sequence of activities. But there is always room for imagination, improvisation, and serendipity. Science and scholarship are human activities and the workflow in all disciplines reflects both convention and innovation.

C. P. Snow's famous idea of the "Two Cultures" is a permanent reminder of how different are the methods of the sciences and the humanities, with, as it is common today to add, the sector called the humanistic social sciences (or HSS). There are risks in speaking of the workflow across the disciplines, particularly when research is more and more specialized. Still, this *Briefing* adopts the shorthand "scholarly workflow" to designate common practices and problems: searching for relevant resources, reading and annotating, managing information overload, reflecting and writing, interacting with colleagues, strategizing publication and dissemination, and more.

Accounts and images of the workflow, based on surveys, interviews, ethnography, and scholarly autobiography, have represented it in different forms, though a circle of steps or stages, repeating itself from project to project, is the most familiar format. The workflow is typically seen as representing orderly progress, or work that gains from habit, a flow whose structure can include the variations that individual scholars bring to it. And today we can add to the workflow uses of the newest digital technologies, like social media, for making work known and for tracking its impact. The workflow is networked, adding a digital dimension at every step.

This *Briefing* identifies the workflow's primary elements. And it names the "digital age" as the circumstances of life and work featuring ubiquitous computing and the networked transformation of communications. Still, digital innovations in the scholarly workflow are being adopted only at a pace determined by the habits, preferences, and expectations of individual scholars. Thus, this *Briefing* includes recognition of a familiar dynamic in the relations of technology and work. The claims of vanguard advocates for the digital remaking of scholarship are fulfilled only unevenly in research experience. Change competes with habit, making individual workflows and the scholarly dispositions they represent as different as the disciplines of inquiry. Studies of the academic generations show that finding the best relations between the old and the new in the workflow, and in the world of scholarly communications that surrounds it, is a project essential to what scholars want in discovery, productivity, and recognition.

Stewart Brand, editor of the famed *Whole Earth Catalog* of the 1960s and then an early Internet enthusiast now credited with inspiring well-known features of the Digital Age, proposed early in this century the distribution of buttons to promote the most thoughtful uses of technology. "Not So Fast," they said, reflecting what would become the sentiment behind social and cultural criticism expressing cautious enthusiasm for forms of digital experience while urging recognition of losses with gains. Such work encourages, as is displayed in this *Briefing*, caution about deterministic assumptions about the technological transformation of all features of our postsecondary educational system, including what is often attributed to the "accelerated academy." For some time we have anticipated the arrival of the "digital scholar." As the *Briefing* shows, such terms are under negotiation as scholars discover in the workflow the extent and meanings of their professional interactions with technology.

The *Briefing* is in two parts representing what scholars of the workflow find to be its characteristics and dilemmas as it is adapted to the digital conditions of academic life. The digital ecosystem is presented as an organizing idea in Part 1, with attention then to essential activities of the workflow, organized according to the common practices and preferences of scholars, and the variable ways it unfolds in research projects. Part 2 looks at how the wish for order and control in the workflow vies with information overload, ceaseless technological innovation, and what some observers see in the acceleration of academic life. In the Conclusion, there are reminders of how in the digital age the workflow is in a new stage of representing what scholars do to advance knowledge and their careers, at the same time it displays the durability of traditional research practices. Finally, readers will find, for a brief book, extensive references. They indicate how the workflow as a subject in scholarly communications takes us to many areas of inquiry, or what is behind the demands of academic research in the digital age.

PART 1

THE WORKFLOW IN ITS PARTS

CHAPTER 1
FROM INFRASTRUCTURE TO ECOSYSTEM

As the digital system of scientific and scholarly communications grew rapidly early in this century, the National Science Foundation (NSF, 2003) and then the American Council of Learned Societies (ACLS, 2006) recognized the emergence of a "cyberinfrastructure," or a network of institutions, people, and technologies that would shape the benefits of electronic inquiry across the disciplines. In its report, the ACLS says,

> The infrastructure of scholarship [meaning the analog one] was built over centuries with the active participation of scholars. The cyberinfrastructure will be built more quickly, and so it is especially important to have broad scholarly participation in its construction: after it is built, it will be much harder to shift, alter, or improve its foundations.
>
> (p. 5)

The warning about "participation" appears to assume that there will be a federally supported "cyberinfrastructure," as it is presented in the NSF report. Of course, that national project has never been realized, although PubMed (the U.S. National Library of Medicine at the National Institutes of Health) is a version of it. The ACLS acknowledges the rapidly growing tangible network and its software applications. But it called for attention to "the more intangible layer of expertise and the best practices, standards, tools, collections and collaborative environments that can be broadly shared across communities of inquiry" (p. 6). Christine Borgman (2007) adopted the term "infrastructure" for her authoritative account of the digital transformation of scholarly communications. But ecology has also gained attention as a fruitful metaphor for an inclusive, pliable, and dynamic view of the whole of the system, particularly in what it suggests in recognition of scholars' interactions with technology among the material elements of their work.

TOWARD AN INTEGRATED VIEW OF RESEARCH PRACTICES

According to Oxford University Internet scholars and theorists Eric Meyer and Ralph Schroeder (2009), "there is no established conceptual apparatus" for representing an "integrated" view of what is before us. To fill the gap, they proposed an ambitious grouping of elements they named an "e-Research Ecosystem"(Figure 1.1). Its scale is what makes it distinctive and even transformative for the scholarly workflow:

> The visibility and dominance of online resources must be seen in a context that is larger than search, fields, and formal and informal scholarly communications. . . . The shift to online resources cannot be left on the level of scholarly communication practices but must be raised to the level of transformation in the very systems of scholarly communication.
>
> (p. 219)

The ecosystem maps a space for communications of all kinds, old and new. Thus, there is still a bottom "layer" designated as "purely offline," or traditional research, including the habits of working with paper. In moving toward what Meyer and Schroeder designate as "purely online," or what in the emerging ecosystem is named "e-Research and e-Discovery," we enact the transformation. The e-Research Ecosystem, a geography (so to speak) of the scholarly workflow, conveys how it feels to be working in our complex and evolving situation, where digital tools are new to many scholars, and where we are likely to see, as is always the case, the impact of innovation side by side with durable habits of inquiry.

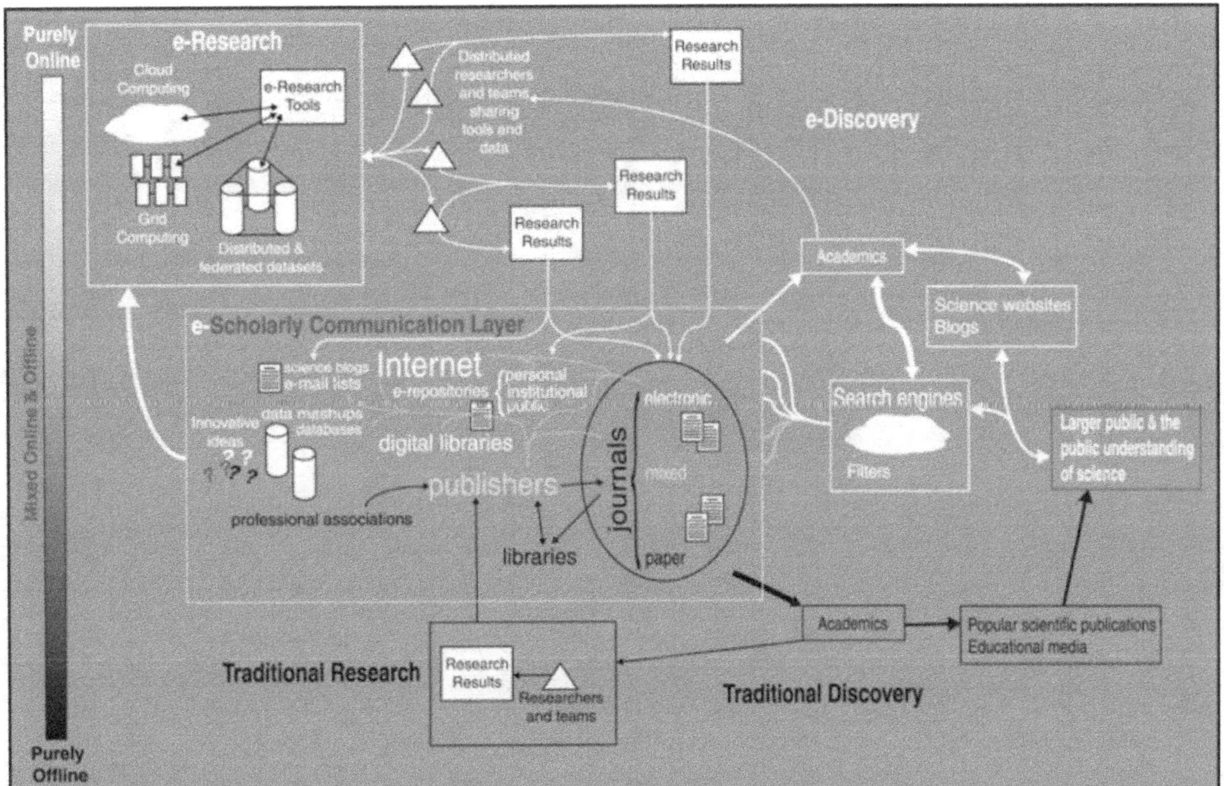

Figure 1.1 The e-Research Ecosystem

Source: Meyer and Schroeder (2009)

A digital research and communications system named an ecosystem relies on a metaphor. The term is defined (in the *Oxford English Dictionary*) as "[a] biological system composed of all the organisms in a particular physical environment, interacting with it and with each other." For some decades, ecological relations among people and the environments in which they live and work, a structure of influences and effects, have been a theme in the social and behavioral sciences, particularly in the study of human development (Elder and Rockwell, 1979). That is the sense in which Meyer and Schroeder use the term, to designate a broad interactive framework for scholarly and scientific work, and communications about it, or what amounts to a bird's-eye perspective.

THE VIEW FROM BELOW

The metaphor is used in an allied if different way by technology and communications scholars Bonnie Nardi and Vicki O'Day (1999), who name "information ecologies" as a way of "looking in the small," or at "locations," like particular organizations or institutions, and units of them, where people use tools and interact with one another. For Nardi and O'Day, it is essential to keep in mind the human scale of the digital transformation, or what the "participants" in a system do: "Designers of tools are responsible for providing useful and clear functionality, but they do not complete the job. As users of tools, we are responsible for integrating them into settings of use in such a way that they make sense to us" (p. 55). The phrase "settings of use" suggests that an ecology of practice refers to the ways scientists and scholars find roles for new tools in the workflow side by side with old ones.

Recognizing that "information ecologies are composed of people, practices, values, and technologies" means seeing them as "opportunistic niches for growth" and places to "use technology with heart." Colleges and universities can be understood in this way. But a "setting" for science and scholarship might also be a unit within a college or university—a college itself (if we are thinking about a university), an academic department, a lab, a research center, or any configuration of researchers shaping the ways that scholars see their informational work.

For the purposes of this *Briefing*, the form that a scientist or scholar gives to their workflow amounts to a personal information ecology. For Nardi and O'Day, being part of an information ecology, even one limited to the practices of a single scholar, means being "intentional" and "reflective" about expectations, methods, and results.

So, the metaphor of ecology applied to the research or informational uses of technology in the workflow can be represented in a view from above (as in a vast e-research ecosystem) and, at the same time at a smaller scale, a view from below of how individuals in particular workplaces manage their relations with tools in an information ecology. The two are complementary. Thus, anyone at work in an information ecology, like a discipline or a post-secondary educational institution, is also a participant in the e-research ecosystem. The model of an information ecology allows for attention to what can be learned about individual encounters with it, and thus favors study of the workflow that features such opportunities.

TECHNOLOGY AT WORK

Depending on what we want to know about what we do in using information and communications technologies, we might favor one or another of the ecological perspectives identified here, or a combination of them. Whatever vocabulary is used to name the context for the workflow and scholarly communications, it must recognize it as more than a mere backdrop or even an environment. Indeed, a comprehensive review of the "context for information behavior" found Nardi and O'Day's information ecologies particularly dynamic, foregrounding human activity more than structure and resources: "Its human and non-human components are tightly interwoven, highly interdependent, constantly evolving" (Courtright, 2007, p. 290).

Such an endorsement suggests how an ecological approach to the scholarly workflow resembles recent attention in organizational studies to the "sociomaterial" approach to understanding the uses of technology at work. According to the influential theorist Wanda Orlikowski (2007), it asks that we abandon our habit of seeing human interactions with machines as if they are still "ontologically separate." In contrast, "the notion of constitutive entanglement presumes that there are no independently existing entities with inherent characteristics. Humans are constituted through relations of materiality—bodies, clothes, food, devices, tools, which, in turn, are produced through human practices" (p. 1438). And these inevitably display the "multiple, messy, complex, and dynamic aspects of technology at work" (Orlikowski, 2010, p. 137). Configured as "information ecology" or "constitutive entanglement," the goal is to study the endless configurations of experience making up the scholarly workflow in the digital age.

CHAPTER 2
CORE ACTIVITIES

An ecological perspective guides us toward seeing the scholarly workflow as an aggregation, if not necessarily a highly ordered system, of closely related activities. With its report on *Scholarly Information Practices in the Online Environment* (SIPOE), the Online Computer Library Center (OCLC) proposed an inclusive format for identifying them. As its authors said, "Scholars and scientists carry out layers of physical and intellectual activity through a complicated mix of mundane and seemingly idiosyncratic tasks that result in a range of immediate and long term outcomes" (Palmer et al., 2009, p. 3).

SIPOE focuses on the activities of disciplines as "scholarly communities." But the study recognizes, as inquiry into information practices in the digital age evolves, the importance of learning more about the subject with attention to the projects and careers of individual researchers. There are many guides to academic research and writing, but only rarely do scholars offer personal accounts of them via managing the research workflow, from the inception of a project through publication (e.g., Abbott, 2014; Ulibarri et al., 2019). Efforts to bring attention to the workflow closer to the experiences of individual scholars are visible in Inputs, Outputs, and Connections (below) and in the account of *A Day in the Life of a (Serious) Researcher* in Chapter 3.

A VOCABULARY FOR THE WORKFLOW

The OCLC project presents the results of empirical studies across the disciplines with a five-part classification of what scholars and scientists do when they are most focused on producing knowledge: searching, collecting, reading, writing, and collaborating. But these "core activities" are complemented by other features of scholarly communications, as an ecological view invites us to recognize the ways that academic research careers are maintained and advanced. The demands are cognitive, reflecting intelligence and insight, and social, reflecting how the work requires interaction with professional colleagues, and with institutions and organizations (like libraries and publishers). Subsequent studies (as in later chapters of this *Briefing*) offer alternative vocabularies for characterizing the scholarly workflow, if with inevitable overlap. But the OCLC account has an important place in the establishment of the workflow in the digital age as an ambitious comprehensive account of information practices. Addressed chiefly to librarians, the goal was to contribute to an understanding of "how to develop effective information resources and tools for scholars."

According to SIPOE, there are sixteen activities or "practices" in the five categories, foundational terms for the workflow. However rarely scholars themselves may think about their work in its parts, OCLC urges librarians to do so in the context of the impact of technology on research.

Core Scholarly Activities

1. **Searching**
   Direct Searching
   Chaining
   Browsing
   Probing
   Accessing
2. **Collecting**
   Gathering
   Organizing
3. **Reading**
   Scanning
   Assessing
   Rereading
4. **Writing**
   Assembling
   Coauthoring
   Disseminating

5. **Collaborating**
   Coordinating
   Networking
   Consulting

Named in its parts in this way, research represents a demanding array of activities. It might be named an "assemblage," to invoke a method from the arts to represent the scholarly workflow. Success requires powers of integration and imagination, or capitalizing on what is learned via the core activities with what might be learned with fresh configurations, in idiosyncratic workflows, of the familiar steps. Thus, another account of the workflow (considered in Chapter 3, "Sequence and Segments") names "brainwork," however difficult to define, as essential for fruitful science and scholarship. The "core activities" named here, however, remind us that scholars and scientists *act* in their research as well as think. And there are what the OCLC team calls "Cross Cutting Primitives" (borrowing the concept from John Unsworth [2000]). These are: monitoring, notetaking, translating, and data practices, and they are used in each of the core activities.

Like all such schemes, SIPOE can make the work look more orderly and even predictable than it generally is. But SIPOE shows what can be gained from seeking as complete a picture of information practices as possible, or a "landscape view," as the study puts it, that may be difficult to see from a day-by-day perspective. The report turns to figurative language to look across disciplinary practices: "Some social scientists, particularly those doing historical and cultural interpretations, are more akin to humanists whose information paths are long, mutable and centrifugal in nature. Quantitative social scientists are more similar to scientists who have more segmented, directed, and centripetal information gathering patterns" (pp. 34–35).

Still, the core activities approach is temporal and it reflects what happens in scholarly communications from the initiation of a research project to the appearance of its results in print or online. "Disseminating" stands for what scholars do in reaching audiences. At the time of its writing, SIPOE could foresee how disseminating research was changing in the digital age. In the years since the extensive expansion of online scholarly communications has made this activity more demanding even if, for example, preprints and other forms of Open Access dissemination now have important roles in completing the workflow.

INPUTS, OUTPUTS, AND CONNECTIONS

The SIPOE approach remains influential. A recent study reflects its selection of practices if with a different way of organizing them. The "model" proposed by Randolph-Macon (VA) College librarian Nancy Falciani-White (2016) features "Inputs" and "Outputs" (categories for most of what we see in SIPOE) and what is done by scholars between the two to integrate them in a research career. The integration is named "gleaning" and defined as "incorporating the connections that naturally occur through collaborations, participation, and simply moving through the day into whatever you happen to be working on" (Booth, 2011, cited in Falciani-White, 2016, p. 123). A question to ask of this "model" is whether it reflects enough of the digital environment, and the institutional or academic context, for scholarly communications.

In 2017, Falciani-White identified the "plethora" of "behaviors"—also in SIPOE—she finds to be typical of productive scholars: skimming, reading, underlining and note-taking, chaining, differentiating, direct searching, browsing, data collection, data analysis, organizing, collaborating, networking, writing, monitoring, presenting, and teaching. There is no particular order because, as is often recognized, the scholarly workflow is fluid and recursive.

SIPOE made these categories familiar in describing the scholarly workflow. But Falciani-White adds the voices of her interview subjects, individualizing essential activities. What activity drew the most intense responses? It was "organizing," which gets more than twice as much space as any other. No one seems satisfied with how they are organizing their rapidly expanding research resources (print and digital). Organizing, as "Personal Information Management" (PIM), is a subject in Chapter 5, "How Much Order Is Enough?"

What is surprising, given developments in scholarly communications since the SIPOE report, is, again, the limited attention Falciani-White gives to the digital context for the research workflow, particularly the transformation of publishing and dissemination. Thus, there is no recognition of the ideals and practices of the Open Access movement and what it may come to represent for dramatic changes in the organization and financing of publishing in journals, or the uses of social media, however problematic the latter may be seen by those who worry about the "Facebooking" of scholarly communications (Nentwich and König, 2014), or the "branding" of academic careers (Duffy and Pooley, 2017).

Still, the "plethora" approach to the workflow, while it represents a small group of research subjects at a single institution, does support other work of the past decade—including "A Day in the Life" (as in Chapter 3, "Sequence and Segments")—that urges caution in assuming that all scholars are keen on joining the digital transformation. Falciani-White (2017) herself says, "While technological changes have resulted in very different research-related tools, the ways in which scholars engage with information as part of their daily work does not seem to have changed substantially over time" (p. 970).

That is a sentiment shared by virtually all those who study the scholarly workflow (e.g., Moore and Singley, 2019). Of course, it is often said that higher education is an institution very slow to change. To what degree that applies to the individual initiative necessary for success in research in the digital age will be visible in the evolving scholarly workflow.

CHAPTER 3
CIRCUIT AND SEGMENTS

A study of the scholarly workflow by Michael Newman and John Sack (2013) of the Stanford University Library featured the transition to electronic publication and how scholars find, store, and retrieve articles. The interviews only occasionally prompted attention to other activities. Sack, the founder of the electronic journal publisher High Wire Press, laments (as in Chapter 7, "Saved by Software") the slow pace in the introduction of digital innovations into the workflow.

In more wide-ranging encounters with scholars, researchers and librarians at Penn State and Cornell have demonstrated why it is hard to identify a common pattern of "information practices," much less "best practices" as they are called in many professional domains. In fact, accounts of information practices among scholars and scientists show that most do *not* have systematic strategies for keeping up to date, capitalizing on all opportunities for discovery, and for organizing and managing their resources.

CIRCUIT OF INQUIRY

As in all areas of life and work, theoretical studies, or those aimed at generalizing about behavior among groups as in SIPOE and allied studies, can be complemented by attention to what scholars and scientists do, or how they account for their day-to-day work in their own words. Ethnographer Smiljana Antonijevic (2015; see also Antonijevic and Cahoy, 2014) offers a model of the research workflow. It includes, inevitably, the SIPOE sequence of categories, if sometimes named differently. But the image of the circuit (Figure 3.1) conveys movement through a regular series of activities with recognition of the recursive character of the work. Search, for example, which necessarily is placed at the beginning, is an ongoing activity, as is reflection, which may appear toward the end of the process but is essential throughout research.

Figure 3.1 reflects ethnographic work based at Penn State but also with scholars at other institutions, particularly in the digital humanities. The results are not, however, as specialized as Antonijevic's focus may suggest. Thus, as she says, the graphical representation was designed as a heuristic device, intended to guide attention to the workflow across the disciplines.

While she recognizes that "knowledge in practice can be hard to articulate or recall," Antonijevic discovers a great deal from her interview subjects and observations. Of course, the workflow is not limited to what is represented

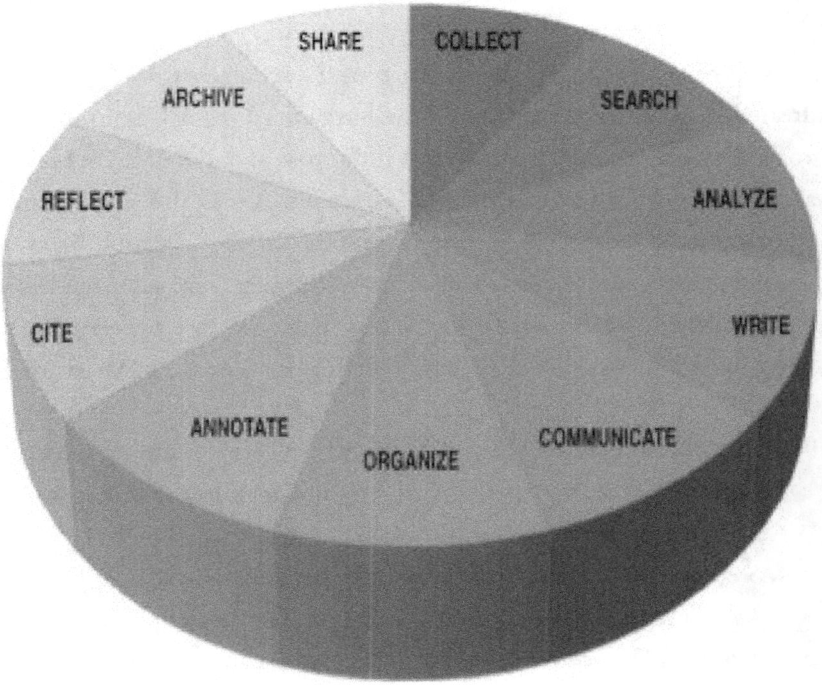

Figure 3.1 The Research Workflow
Source: Antonijevic (2015)

in the figure. An example would be what is said of "reflection," presented by Antonijevic as a feature of reading, associated with "annotating" texts. Reading itself does not actually appear in the scheme, though there are several places in which it is the foundation of the task that is named. In any case, most scholars are reflecting, in one form or another, at all stages of their work. So, while workflow sounds linear and unidirectional, different elements appear and reappear as needed in the life of a research project. Scholars don't do all of their searching at the start but continue to discover useful work as a project unfolds.

Inevitably, an important lesson Antonijevic learns is that each phase of research influences the others in ways that are not always predictable. That prompts her to say: "Digital research tools should be designed to support a continuous research workflow, enabling scholars to navigate among separate, yet interconnected activities" (p. 53). Others have registered the roles of browsing and encounters with the unexpected (as in Chapter 4, "Search and Serendipity").

LINEAR AND CHAOTIC

Questions of navigation among the parts of the scholarly workflow are also addressed in an unusual study at Cornell organized in "A Day in the Life" format (Tancheva et al., 2016; see also Eldermire and Tang, 2016; Gessner et al., 2017). But a circle or sequence is only implicit in this work. Instead the librarian researchers favor nine "segments" of the "research lifecycle" presented in self-reported ratios of attention they get from scholars. In recognition of the recursive nature of the segments, they are presented without any signs of temporal order (based on Tancheva et al., 2016, p. 14):

- *Academic Activities:* Note-taking, writing (including production, editing, formatting, etc.), managing information (including storing information), and field or lab work.
- *Seeking Information*: Searching for academic and nonacademic purposes.
- *Library Resources:* Using library resources, online and physical.
- *Self-discipline/Self-management*: Managing habits, motivation, and distractions.
- *Space:* The work environment—location, space, setup, furnishings, light, and more.

- *Circum-academic Activities*: Professional networking, conference participation, using social media for academic purposes.
- *Obstacles*: Managing interruptions in research work, problems in accessing resources.
- *Brainwork:* Thinking and sensemaking, or what goes into understanding a problem and organizing and presenting research and new knowledge about it.
- *Technology*: Its presence or absence, specific hardware or software, online resources, and social media.

To a degree, the categories overlap with Antonijevic's, as in "Academic Activities" and "Seeking Information," with annotating, writing, and archiving. But the format includes broad forms of scholarly behavior like "Self-Discipline" and "Brainwork," each an activity that cannot be represented as an independent segment of a workflow sequence. The "lifecycle" also recognizes "Obstacles" to steady research and the meanings of "Space," or the impact of the work environment, from campus offices, to coffee shops, to home. Each of these four categories of the workflow merits recognition beyond what is named in SIPOE as "core activities." For example, "themes that emerged regarding brainwork included the relationship between writing longhand and deep thinking, strategies that interviewees used to enhance motivation or avoid cognitive depletion, different environmental or time-of-day preferences for 'mindless' work and work that requires real thought, and the need to eliminate technology to focus" (p. 25).

The Cornell team interviewed a small sample of faculty and graduate students in several disciplines after they had each kept a detailed record of their workflow over the course of a typical workday (if there is one at a research university). The study was based on these records and follow-up interviews where subjects addressed questions about the impact of digital innovation and the roles of libraries. The focus throughout was on going beyond library-based studies of information practices, or seeing them and allied pursuits "in the context of other components that [librarians] normally do not see or know about" (p. 35). Still, in its design the study plainly represented what the Cornell librarians had been observing in their interactions with the faculty and graduate students. Thus, "technological innovation has increased the extent to which individuals can adjust available tools to suit their personal preferences" (p. 39).

TASK NEGOTIATION

It is surely no surprise that the Stanford, Penn State, and Cornell studies of the scholarly workflow found that individual differences matter more than anything else. They can reflect disciplinary conventions, personal histories and preferences, and a configuration of opportunities and resistances, or even refusals, in encounters with digital innovations.

The Cornell study demonstrated that "research begins everywhere" (Gessner et al., 2017, p. 542), that it is "interrupted and yet continuous," and that it is "simultaneously linear, in its overarching goal from idea to manuscript, and chaotic," as researchers constantly negotiate tasks and move among activities (p. 535). As Antonijevic found at Penn State, practices are highly "idiosyncratic." The Cornell study names "task negotiation" as the frequent stance of scholars looking for ways in and out of segments of the workflow, adapting as they go to opportunities and to variable intensity in one or another segment as demands (as in publication and grant proposal deadlines) and mood require. Accordingly, interviews are coded for "Self-Discipline" and "Brainwork," or orientations to research that influence how it is done without specifying a discrete step in the process.

Inevitably, scholarly practices can belie the structure conveyed by any orderly looking image of the workflow. Segments count more than sequence and scholarly personality plays as big a role as commitment to the process (see also Acord and Harley, 2013). The example of writing can show what may be missed in a focus on visible actions in scholarly work. Thus, "not writing," or the routines (as "brainwork") that many successful academic authors count as essential before they are actually in front of a computer screen, is hard to locate in current ways of representing the workflow (Cloutier, 2016).

ONE MORE CIRCLE

A Day in the Life also presents a compact image of the workflow, gathering its nine segments into three main "spheres of practice": the process of research, academic networking, and managing the self (p. 35). But another recent representation of the workflow is again in the form of a circuit or circle. Described by a writer at *Inside Higher Ed* as a "mandala" or symbol of the search for completeness and unity (McLemee, 2015), the *101 Innovations in Scholarly Communications* project at the University of Utrecht relies on a sequence of familiar categories: discovery, analysis, writing, publication, outreach, and assessment. They are named as locations for the uses of hundreds of digital tools, an "ecosystem" of them, classified according to styles of scholarly and scientific work as the sequence unfolds (adapted from Bosman and Kramer [2015]):

- *Traditional* tools add no functionality compared to print era, except online accessibility.
- *Modern* tools use scale and linking possibilities of the internet to increase speed and efficiency.
- *Innovative* tools change "the ways its always been done"—for example, user-driven, different business models, changes in the sequence of research activities, shifting stakeholder roles.
- *Experimental* tools represent radical change, with sometimes uncertain technologies and outcomes, still under development.

The format reflects the FORCE11 initiative on behalf of the digital transformation of the workflow (as in Chapter 7, "Saved by Software?"). Still, without the "in-depth studies" promised by the Utrecht team it is hard to know how likely it is that the transformed workflow will display the app-based "interoperability" that will bind what they see as an emerging digital ecosystem. Other representations of the workflow, where they distinguish among the uses of technology, recognize the fruitful ways that scholars find compatibility among old and new tools.

CHAPTER 4
SEARCH AND SERENDIPITY

Search is an information practice that is essential to research success, guiding a scholar toward relations between prior and new work. Search takes us to timely and relevant articles and books, but it also helps us to see the contours of a subject, and sometimes of a field itself. And then, as ambition or curiosity dictates, we find resources adjacent to where we began. Thus, Google Scholar advises users, presumably even its experienced academic ones: "Explore! There's rarely a single answer to a research question." Electronic searching not only speeds the workflow but, whatever the limits of Google Scholar's proprietary algorithm, it also expands it in helping to bring about new kinds of interdisciplinary projects.

Named as the first in SIPOE's "Core Activities," search is a "complex and interactive process," even though it is, nominally, most important at the opening stages of research. Carol Palmer and her colleagues (2009) acknowledge one potential cost of digital age abundance: "In an online environment searchers tend to work more quickly and less deeply [than in traditional print-based searches]" (p. 11). But the section on search in *Scholarly Information Practices in the Online Environment* shows how going beyond direct searching allows for ambitious configurations of "chaining," "probing," and "browsing." Indeed, in a 2019 study of how scholars find what they use, 33 percent said that it was with browsing, while only 29 percent did so with direct searching. Another 18 percent reported relying on work cited in an article (Tenopir, Christian, and Kaufman, 2019).

And then there are the scholars whose success at searching includes a resource that escapes survey research. A sociologist reports:

> I wanted to hire a research assistant to go through newspaper and other media material for a specific project. He asked me: so, what should I be looking for? I answered: "Look for interesting stuff." Then I realized I couldn't tell him more. Now that I have worked with the material myself for some time I could go back and be more specific, but then I relied more on a gut feeling, that couldn't really be converted into clear instructions.
>
> (cited in Lofgren, 2014, p. 81)

GOOGLE SCHOLAR

As publication began moving online, digital databases (representing fields of inquiry or collections of journals) at the websites of academic libraries still guided researchers to new and archived work. But in 2004 Google introduced Google Scholar, which quickly had a galvanizing effect on search, particularly, as Google itself emphasized when it announced the service, for what it offers in consolidating different locations for identifying useful resources. It is now by far the most comprehensive academic search engine (Gusenbauer, 2019) and U.S. scholars increasingly turn to it alongside scholarly databases (Blankstein and Wolff-Eisenberg, 2019).

Researchers appear to have confidence in the proprietary Google algorithm that orders the search results by ranking documents, presumably as scholars do, with recognition of the author, the place of publication, and how often and how recently it has been cited in the literature. In their account of Google, Nentwich and König (2014) acknowledge its uses but they note that authors, with little choice, have acquiesced to a ranking system of online presentation that is actually unknown to them (see also Wellmon, 2016).

When it was launched, there was concern among academic librarians that Google Search would replace the traditional scholarly databases and ultimately make libraries less useful to faculty and students. That is what has happened, as is made plain in the account by David Nicholas and David Clark (2015) of "Finding Stuff." University libraries now include Google Scholar among their search tools, many with advice about using it, while some urge caution in relying on it without consulting library-based databases. According to one research university library,

> Google Scholar is useful as a jumping off point for your research, but to do in-depth research, you need to use a subject specific database provided by the university library. Google Scholar currently lacks the ability to easily focus your search with features that are specifically designed for a given discipline.

This library says that "highly developed subject databases are a much better choice [for] reliable access and sophisticated search techniques."

Such cautions can direct us to an unanticipated consequence of Google Scholar, and perhaps of digital search generally. But, as Nicholas and Clark explain, the service dominates search, representing speed and reach in the task, and more autonomy for scholars: "Libraries have been disintermediated and marginalized as a result of the digital transition. Information do-it-yourself has become the norm and Google and the like have helped to accelerate the process by providing a search facility par excellence." In effect, Nicholas and Clark claim, "We are all librarians now" (p. 22) if in a manner that hardly suits traditional images of search. Thus, Google Scholar often serves the common style of online behavior, or impatient "skittering" and "grabbing information snippets" (p. 32).

Like others, Nicholas and Clark worry about the impact of easy and rapid digital search on reading for everyone whose work is with texts (see also Nicholas and Clark, 2012). An allied problem with the ease of search is profligate downloading and what that presents for effective storing, managing, and using resources. No doubt some expressions of anxiety about information overload reflect what scholars impose on themselves in unmet aspirations for reading. Search and stockpiling go together.

STRATEGIC READING

For some observers of the workflow, Google Scholar can do more to speed it up. To celebrate its tenth anniversary in 2014, Google Scholar (at its blog) ran a series of statements by users and others knowledgeable about search. John Sack devoted his contribution to what he found missing in Google Scholar: aids to reading displayed articles faster. That would mean helping readers bypass the text as a whole in favor of attention to what the search process determines are the most relevant paragraphs, or to the tables and other presentations of figures. Sack says what many claim who study scientific reading habits today. That is, most scientists skim in their reading, or read only "strategically," interested in but a few parts of any article. If Sack and like-minded admirers of Google have their way, the future of Google for the workflow will be in how scholars use what they find.

Relying on Google Scholar for academic searching has also had an impact on citation patterns in scholarship and science. In a study that has had considerable attention, James Evans (2008) demonstrated that the very structure of Google Scholar and how it is often used—in haste and with insufficient regard for older sources and for the range of available online work—means that electronic publication shows signs of being "narrow" in its representation of the research literature.

Asked on its tenth anniversary about what he would like to see Google Scholar be able to do in the years ahead, founder Anurag Archaya said,

> We are very good at helping people to find the articles they are looking for and can describe. But the next big thing we would like to do is to get you the articles that you need, but that you don't know to search for. Can we make serendipity easier? How can we help everyone to operate at the research frontier without them having to scan over hundreds of papers—a very inefficient way of finding things—and do nothing else all day long?
>
> (cited in Van Noorden, 2014)

FROM INTENTION TO ACCIDENT

Being purposeful or well-focused is a useful trait in pursuing research, as in other activities. After all, scholarship and science reflect the goal of gaining knowledge of the world and experience, a rational enterprise. Still, Carole Palmer and her colleagues in *Scholarly Information Practices in the Online Environment* recognize browsing as a desirable feature of search, acknowledging what it can mean for serendipitous discovery. Scholars and scientists who browse suspend their determination to stay as close as possible to an original object of search and adopt a different cognitive stance. "Because browsing tends to be broad and flexible, scholars encounter materials that would not be found through searching or chaining, and the new information may stimulate unexpected and fortuitous intellectual connections" (p. 14). Of course, browsing is typically associated with what can be done in scanning the shelves at a library, which scholars now visit only occasionally. Still a recently proposed "typology" of browsing styles comes with proposals for software applications that would make browsers of scholars sitting at screens (McKay et al., 2019).

There is hope that browsing in any format can be more than a casual habit. It is precisely because browsing can yield more than the unexpected—the "unknown unknowns" according to Nicholas and Clark (2015, p. 29)—that scholars of information practices have theorized what appears to resist systematic inquiry. Can we study and understand what comes unplanned to research projects? Stephann Makri and Ann Blandford (2012) believe there is a "recipe" for fruitful serendipity. They organize it as a "process" with a sequence of stages that feature the cognitive work, in "projecting," "reflecting," and "considering," and then making something of the unexpected.

We come across an illuminating article or book by accident, or we have an encounter (at a conference, for example) with a like-minded scholar or scientist unknown to us who can offer a fresh perspective on a problem that won't yield to our own studies. A laboratory accident leads to unanticipated knowledge. From there learning in this manner is simple, if we are open to surprise, "through an iterative process of projecting value from an [unexpected cognitive connection], continuing to exploit the connection, and reflecting on the value of the outcome" (Makri and Blandford, 2012, p. 692).

In effect, reflection and interpretation, well within the habits of scholars and scientists, are resources for capitalizing on what may (at first) surprise us, as we browse in the literature or go about our daily business in the conduct of research. In effect, the merely unexpected becomes the serendipitous because a scholar or scientist is thinking as one, or staying within the role of researcher. That entails identifying the value of the unexpected as its role in a research project becomes clear.

Of course, what is unplanned cannot be incorporated in advance into the research workflow. And the workflow itself, when guided by aims of efficiency as they are encouraged by advocates of more technology, can be an obstacle to the benefits of serendipity. Thus, study of the serendipitous in research shows that such incidents should be seen as more than happy accidents. "Mechanisms of serendipity" circulate irregularly in the workflow but, paradoxically, according to patterns of fruitful deviance from research routines:

> Serendipity may become conspicuous because the growth of theory makes it stand out to any given observer, or serendipity may be observable only to some with certain tools, techniques, and attributes, or serendipity may emerge following methodological deviations, errors, and spillages, or serendipity may involve a network of actors.
>
> (Yaqub, 2018, p. 172)

More precision in identifying forms of serendipity, paradoxically enough, reminds us of how a pliable workflow can itself be resource for scholarly learning.

PART 2

CONDITIONS OF CONTROL

CHAPTER 5
HOW MUCH ORDER IS ENOUGH?

Apple products are known for their streamlined or clean design but Steve Jobs's home office was apparently always in disarray. The cluttered versus the neat workspace is a familiar form of personal expression, with partisans of each wondering how colleagues at work can thrive in a manner the opposite of their own. Of course, a scholar's workflow can't be separated from its physical conditions, however much we feel ourselves at work in cyberspace.

CONSTRUCTIVE CHAOS

Most scholars want to be better organized than they are. But there are holdouts, reflecting the gap between desires and practices. An unusual feature in the *University of Chicago Magazine*—representing an institution famed for the rigors of its scholarship—presented in photographs a selection of the messiest offices on campus (Yoe, 2001). The "Kings of Chaos" who we see were also among Chicago's most famous and influential professors, like the legal scholar Cass Sunstein, now at Harvard. The floor of his office is entirely covered by books and articles, with a necktie hanging over the arm of a chair.

A consoling book celebrates what the University of Chicago photographs display with amusement. In *A Perfect Mess: The Hidden Benefits of Disorder* (2007), Eric Abrahamson and David Freedman assert that "[i]t takes extra effort to neaten up a system" and that, as we might expect, disorder (in the form of the messy desk and files on the floor) can be quite functional for adults in many different kinds of work. Recent empirical studies support the association of disorder with creativity, if with some cautions about its applicability across all domains of human activity, like a hospital operating room. Organizational psychologist Kathleen Vohs (2013), acknowledging the minimalist trend in office design, says, "While cleaning up certainly has its benefits, clean spaces might be too conventional to let inspiration flow." At the very least, Vohs says, on the basis of other experiments on the effects of the orderliness of space on thinking, we can say that they "include a range of normative and nonnormative outcomes." Still, she proposes, "Disorderly environments seem to inspire breaking free of tradition, which can produce fresh insights" (Vohs, Redden, and Rahinel, 2014, p. 1866; see also Kim and Zhong, 2017).

Being in the insight business, so to speak, scientists and scholars are plainly candidates for managing the research workflow in local conditions that would please Sunstein. A physicist and University of Chicago colleague found near magical qualities in the "star stuff" cluttering his office: "One of the things that we all try to do is avoid thinking linearly. Having a messy desk helps to do that. It provides the odd connection. It's constructive chaos" (cited in Yoe, 2001).

PROBLEMS OF PMSI

Scholars are always seeking better ways to keep track of the print and digital resources essential for their research. Cornell is another leading research university. Should we assume that a study of its scholars would show them to be experts at organizing the resources they need to do their work, and wary of any lack of order? An inquiry into academic habits of information management at Cornell (it preceded the "Day in the Life" study considered in Chapter 3) concluded that the best way, and the most tactful, to describe them was "idiosyncratic," in forms of personal management of scholarly information (PMSI) representing in the acronym the pioneering work on Personal Information Management, or PIM, by William Jones (2007).

Organizing analog and digital resources varies from field to field, reflecting roles for quantitative data, documents, images, and more, and the preferences of individual scholars. Thus, Frank Sinatra's famous performance of "My Way" suggests just how strongly most scholars and scientists believe in the very personal approach they take to managing their files—although for some the file itself can be a challenging format.

Cornell librarians Kaila Bussert, Kathy Chiang, and Kornelia Tancheva (2011) make plain what most scholars and scientists know, or what they encounter in digital search: "The ease with which researchers can download ten thousand articles into their computers and print hundreds of them is both a blessing and a curse" (p. 126). We have ready access to many more sources than had been the case when print dominated communications, and the low cost of digital "saving" multiplies problems of classification and storage—and the efficient use of what search reveals. Still, every workflow needs "some sort of personal information space with signposts for recognition and retrieval" (p. 127).

What do the scholars and scientists that Bussert and her colleagues studied—with interviews and office visits to observe firsthand what work spaces looked like—actually do to organize their files? The best answer might be "[a] bit of everything," reflecting habits and preferences that work best given the specialized tasks of research. Need defines the way that research information is managed on the personal level. Despite the availability of many new tools, like digital bookmarking and reference systems like EndNote, most subjects of the study found that these can "complicate" information management. And the Cornell research reminds us of complications even in the physical space of the scholarly workflow: "In the 360-degree scan of the [faculty participants] offices the scholars were very specific about objects nearby but less so about the contents of cabinets and shelves across the office" (p. 134). But a misplaced document is only an occasion for learning, or as one subject says of repeat visits to online journals: "If I can't find something I just read it again and that's usually useful anyways. . . . that's my system" (p. 142).

Paradoxically perhaps, it looks like print will have a long life in scholarship and science given the lack of satisfying ways of taking and storing notes (in many forms) on digital texts. This isn't to say, though, that scholars and scientists don't change over time in how they manage information, adopting, in personal and often idiosyncratic ways, features of new technology even while they stay loyal to well-worn styles for doing their work, as Terje

Hillesund (2010) has also documented. The Cornell study reached a similar conclusion:

> The most salient feature of information that defines the way that it is managed by serious researchers is its fragmentation across platforms, formats and locations. Contrary to our expectations, even though this presents an inconvenience, most [subjects in the Cornell study] appeared to accept information fragmentation in stride and to have devised ways of dealing with it.
>
> (p. 147)

And so too do Cornell's graduate students. One told Bussert, expressing a common academic wish: "I want to make my library so that it's all in one place, so that I have access to all of my stuff in one place and I don't have to remember, 'Oh this one was on paper only and is on my desk at home, or in the office'." Alas, it appears to be a forlorn hope among most of the faculty researchers, not that they haven't made an effort to make effective practices their own: "I always find that if I try and impose a system that other people have used. . . . it doesn't work for me because I have my own way of doing my information management. And so *this is what works for me*" (p. 140, emphasis added).

A MODEL FOR MANAGING

Competing images of PMSI (even when not calling it that) focus on the intentionality that scholars can bring to the workflow as a scene of personal scholarly archive building (Marshall, 2008). The Cornell scholars varied in how systematic they sought to be in organizing and storing research resources. The librarian scholars at Cornell supported their workflow autonomy, however idiosyncratic in its PMSI. For Ellysa Cahoy (2013), studying the workflow at Penn State (e.g., in her collaboration with Smiljana Antonijevic [2014]), there is only one choice, an orderly and complete archive.

> The scholar's workbench is crowded with many disparate tools, devices, and information collections. In order for intentional, sustained self-archiving to occur, users must learn how to draw together, assess, manage, and archive the most important scholarly materials in their dispersed collections.
>
> (p. 149)

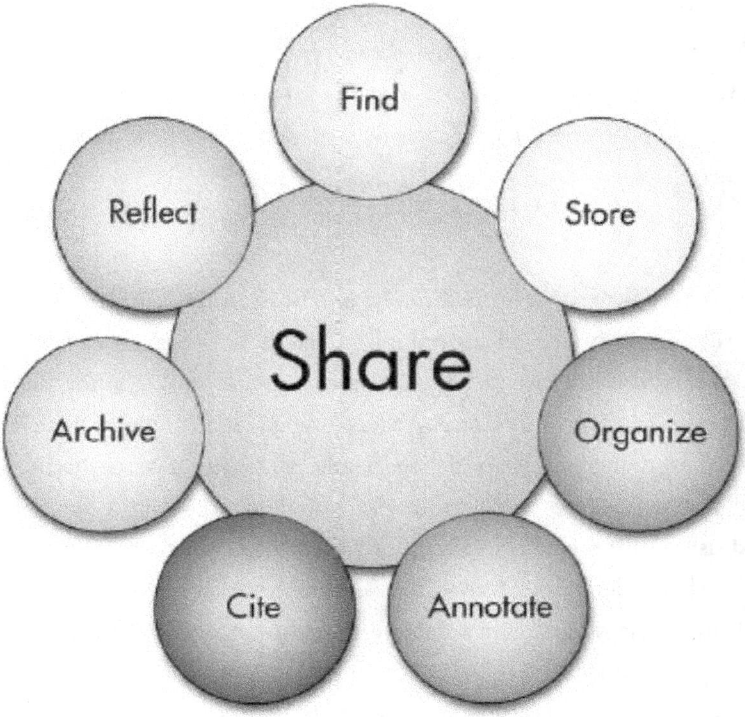

Figure 5.1 The Information Management, Creation, Sharing, and Archiving Model
Source: Cahoy (2013)

The path toward integration into their research of sustained archival practices can reflect faculty collaboration with librarians in identifying and practicing "critical digital literacies" (or an "architecture") for scholarly management of the online workflow. A "guiding model" (Figure 5.1) is meant to suggest "the unification of all stages of the research life cycle."

Still, Cahoy's optimism about the appeal of a workflow "model" belies what the Cornell researchers found among their subjects, and what ethnographers of research find when they get close to working scholars (e.g., Hillesund, 2010; Lofgren, 2014).

SCHOLARLY WORKFLOW AS BRICOLAGE

In an anomaly, Cahoy recently joined again with Smiljana Antonijevic in identifying how unruly and yet productive the workflow can be for humanities and some social science scholars.

> For [them], storing and organizing their research materials is not a technical or an information science activity. It is a deeply personal intellectual pursuit of organizing their thoughts in a way that supports a subjective process of knowledge production, and enables them to construct digital workflows as bricolage.
>
> (Antonijevic and Cahoy, 2018, para 38)

The now well-known term "bricolage" (Johnson, 2012) came into scholarly discourse from the anthropologist Claude Levi Strauss's observations of mythical thinking and the ways it reuses materials at hand. Plans can yield to chance, and results often reflect unexpected scholarly associations: "While the engineer uses specialized tools adjusting tasks to [their] availability and striving for perfection, the bricoleur takes the opposite route and adjusts non-specialized tools to a variety of tasks, tolerating imperfection. The bricoleur achieves that by combining available tools and resources into an improvised aggregate adjusted to his or her needs" (Antonijevic and Cahoy, 2018, para 53).

But bricolage as a method is far from the workflow symmetries of any "archiving model" (Lambotte and Meunier, 2013). It accepts disorder as a necessary element of the process. That is what Andrew Abbott (2014) urges young scholars to recognize as the essence of the scholarly workflow: "From a nonlinear body of research—some of it orderly and rational, much of it chaotic and contingent, all of it loosely tied together—[will] come a clear argument" (p. 35). Speaking as a highly productive sociologist, Abbott says that clarity comes about as a project "gradually turns itself linear by mutually adjusting all of its parts as they develop in parallel" (p. 219).

The adjustments, of course, are human actions representing personal aspirations. Side by side with efforts to make the scholarly workflow a systematic enterprise, and now for some observers with more digitally supported order, there has been recognition that what matters as much as how any scholarly work is done is who is doing it, or what the workflow represents in experience and professional disposition. A study led by Joseph Kaye (2006) of forty-eight scholars in many fields found that PIM, and particularly personal archiving, is "not only about efficient storage and retrieval of information."

The stakes can be higher. Archiving is "used as an expression and crafting of identity, projected outward towards the world as well as back at the individual to reinforce his or her sense of self." Thus, archives have a role in a researcher's "construction and maintenance of identity" (p. 279).

CHAPTER 6

INFORMATION OVERLOAD, ONCE MORE

Fewer and fewer scholars today know what it took before digitization to search confidently if not exhaustively in an academic library. An unusual record of the transition from print to screens is an account by historian David Bell (2005) of his first encounters with the products of online search. Instant access to obscure resources now digitized prompts this assessment of the emerging conditions of the scholarly workflow: "Name your keyword, and the Internet delivers the citations to you with the force of a fire hose in the face" (p. 28). Bell's recognition of his new research situation reflects the attention in our culture to the problem of too much information (e.g., Gleick, 2011; Levitin, 2014).

In their account of online search as "Finding Stuff," David Nicholas and David Clark (2015) acknowledge that online research typically yields more than we know exists or even want. But they assert that "[t]he sheer benefits of unparalleled and unlimited access to information are so great that they more than compensate for any problems that arise from an overabundance of irrelevant, poor, or mediocre information." They cite a scholar who told them that he "preferred to have problems with information management rather than problems with information retrieval" (pp. 26–27).

A PERENNIAL PROBLEM

Digital access to scholarly and scientific resources makes everyone feel like they will never catch up with work important to their research. But information overload isn't a new phenomenon. The Roman philosopher and statesman Seneca believed that "[a]n abundance of books is a distraction." Of course, Seneca was thinking about scrolls, the form of the book in the time that he lived. But even as scrolls became more widely accessible, what worried him was growing superficiality in reading. He urged the readers, as few as there were in his time, not to collect too many books and instead concentrate on the best.

Seneca is quoted by historian Ann Blair in her acclaimed book on the "information explosion" in Europe in the sixteenth and seventeenth centuries: *Too Much to Know: Managing Scholarly Information before the Modern Age* (2011). Efforts to manage information overload were a crucial feature of the scholarly and scientific worlds of the first centuries of printed books. Blair shows that as books and other forms of print began to circulate widely, readers had to invent new ways to manage information, some internal to texts like the table of contents and the index, and some external, or books about books classifying and summarizing them.

In an interview Blair offers a surprise, noting that as we continue to struggle with keeping track of all the information and knowledge now available she herself relies on her memory as a "crucial player" (Golden, 2011). That certainly differs from those who suggest that memory is not so important anymore when we can simply go to the Internet to find out anything we want to know (as in "Just Google it").

Even before research began to appear in digital form, twentieth-century scholars and scientists battled overload with the specialized format of the "annual review." These have been for many decades authoritative accounts of recent work in significant subjects organized by discipline. Annual Reviews (2011), the publishing company that has represented this approach to keeping up, itself surveyed early career scholars and scientists in order to identify its role in managing information overload. Not surprisingly, the format of the annual review was found to be a most timely resource for making the most of the flood of articles and books. There is no mystery there, as Blair suggests, in specifying "selecting and summarizing" as essential information practices.

Still, the problem that Blair and other historians of reading face is whether the digital age presents a set of truly unprecedented conditions for managing information. Within the categories of storing, sorting, and selecting and summarizing that interest Blair and others, can enough be done to turn the tide? Information sobriety (so to speak) may be one answer, for, as experts on search remind us, "the astonishing level of access has made us drunk in information terms" (Nicholas and Clark, 2015, p. 23). The problem, again, is the apparent willingness of researchers to accept problems of overload as a by-product of having so much at hand.

DARK TO LIGHT

Can the difficulties be addressed? One resource is familiar. According to Chad Wellmon (2015), the modern research university in Germany was designed to help manage the flood of publication in all fields of knowledge. It promoted in the curriculum and the classroom, and in the kinds of scholarly projects identified by Ann Blair, discriminating and integrative reading. In effect, scholars are managing information overload all the time in curriculum development and teaching. Commonly seen as distinctive enterprises, teaching and scholarship do not together present themselves as offering a strategy for managing information overload. But Wellmon's approach suggests how more attention to syllabus design can be a resource for understanding what can be made of selective attention. In any case, more technology may not be the answer. "Search technologies facilitate but do not replace the messy, context-bound, all-too-human creation of knowledge" (Wellmon, 2016, p. 119).

Of course, it has been centuries since anyone had anything close to complete knowledge of a subject via what had been written about it. David Bawden and Lyn Robinson (2009, 2020) have made plain the scale of the problem while they advise on managing it. Thus, an important effect of the screen and Web browser is to remove the "look and feel" of differences among resources, with "homogenized diversity" adding to our sense of feeling overwhelmed, or of having lost control of essential forms of information practice. So, "losing control" is one way of charactering the anxiety we feel, or the "dark side" of the benefits that have come with technology.

The study of information overload shows that it is experienced in different ways. Thus, for Bawden and Robinson, as for others, scholarly use of information is individual and shaped by context. What some scholars find as overload, others welcome as opportunity (or even "lifeblood"). Bawden and

Robinson endorse the idea of "personal information style" as the best resource for facing "information anxiety." And they name the strategy of "satisficing" (borrowed from the great economist Herbert Simon), or "taking just enough information to meet a need." Still, it may be understandable that where the goal is expert knowledge and the stakes may be very high, in medical research for example, that a scholar or scientist would be uneasy about settling for less than knowing everything about a problem.

It is easy to see why Bawden and Robinson, mindful of the "dark side" of information abundance, make attention to "information practices" essential as long as we face a steady stream of change in our information technologies. In effect, scholars and scientists in all disciplines and fields need to understand their relation to information, and in particular what rapid and continuing advances in technology mean for how they go about their work. Education and science writer Elizabeth Gibney (2014) summarizes digital services that scholars and scientists might turn to gain more control of their resources. She reminds us of the many thousands of papers that are published every day. Without invoking artificial intelligence (AI) (as others might) for the transformation of scholarly communications, she asks about turning to "machine learning" so that software can guide researchers toward what is likely to interest them. Still, Gibney quotes a geneticist who is very up-to-date in his digital information practices but who believes that relying on a machine to customize suggestions can mean "blinders on your intellectual scope." He notes too, in accord with an academic sentiment often observable in this *Briefing*, the strategy he favors: "It's working for me, and that's all that matters" (p. 130).

MAKING READERS SMARTER

Are there principles to be observed? In an account of the "bright side of information," counterpoint to Bawden and Robinson, Tibor Koltay (2017) advocates "mitigating" the problems presented by information overload. He urges more scholarly or research agency, or attention to our habits of PIM, a familiar strategy among information scientists and librarians. It features what amounts to what psychologists would call "meta-cognition" about OCLC's "Core Activities" (as in Chapter 2).

But Koltay asks for more. First, we need better *information architecture*, or the design (or redesign) of the systems we rely on. "Ill-structured, unclear information causes information overload. However, if we can improve the conciseness, consistency, and comprehensibility of information, the level of information-processing capacity of the individual can increase" (p. 768). This will be no easy task. It will require among designers "deep understanding of information users." But we know how many kinds there are, even in the scholarly world.

Second, after any technological (or design) solution attention goes to capacities and habits of information users who can best manage information overload with "critical reading" and "critical thinking." Koltay urges more attention to "information literacy" because "what is digital is also subject to human agency and to human understanding." But Koltay prefers the phrase *information fluency*, or "conceptual understanding of, and ability to adapt to, changing information environments, ecologies, and contexts." Thus, someone who is fluent in this way "possesses integrated technological skills and understanding about finding, using, and reusing information and knowledge in the networked digital age" (p. 770). Accordingly, *information fluency* "focuses on understanding, rather than skills or competencies." Questions remain, though, about how discipline specific it must be and whether a separate category is needed for "data literacy."

As Koltay says, information overload has "many faces," making it a difficult problem to manage. Bawden and Robinson recognize as much in their latest review of our situation and "coping strategies." Solutions lie in attention to the workflow itself: "The people, and the mechanism, which suffer from overload are by and large the same as those which cause it" Bawden and Robinson, 2020). Though he wants more from the infrastructure (or the "e-Research Ecosystem"), Koltay urges a more deliberate approach rooted in what scholars can do for themselves, in effect making the most of activity within the scholarly workflow as a local information ecology. Thus, AI will not solve the problem: "It is better to make people smarter instead of producing smarter computers" (p. 773).

CHAPTER 7
SAVED BY SOFTWARE?

Workflow studies reveal surprising ambivalence among researchers about the uses of technology. Virtually all welcome digital access to journals and articles, while many remain uncertain about e-books (Blummer and Kenton, 2018). Beyond that, as is shown in Ithaka S+R studies (*A Day in the Life* and its ongoing series on "changing research practices" in the disciplines), the record of adoption of technology at all steps in the workflow is uneven.

PENCILS AND PIXELS

As noted earlier (in Chapter 3, "Circuit and Segments"), the *101 Innovations in Scholarly Communications* initiative underway at the library of the University of Utrecht, with its circular representation of the workflow, was designed to feature the steady adoption of new software. Hundreds of apps are allocated to the six categories of the Utrecht visualization of the research cycle. For organizers Bosman and Kramer (2015), scholars must "know whether using a new tool will reduce time needed to get desired results or even get results that were hitherto impossible to get." But making such judgments isn't easy and the proliferation of tools from many sources and moving among them make interoperability essential. Librarians know about what the major journal publishers do to enlarge their roles in digital collections. Bosman and Kramer favor the expansion of digital applications to scholarly work but they offer a timely caution: "Researchers like an efficient workflow, but big players are also taking a workflow/ecosystem view to developing their portfolio of tools."

The survey and graphical representation of the results in the *101 Innovations* project show one way of looking at the adoption of innovative software for the workflow. As interview-based and ethnographic studies reveal, many scholars are diffident about the constant stream of new apps and cling to the most familiar forms of digital and professional communications. The Cornell group in *A Day in the Life* reports that "e-mail is used by everyone, everywhere" (Tancheva et al., 2016, p. 24). For Antonijevic (2015), "e-mail is a killer app" (p. 61). But everyone who studies the scholarly workflow encounters pockets of indifference. There are those who still rely on printing anything worth storing or on making a digital file on a flash drive. And a historian told Antonijevic: "I am a dinosaur. Everybody at the library has their laptop and they go 'click, click, click.' I have reams of paper and lots of pencils" (p. 56).

As Terje Hillesund's (2010) inventive study of scholars at work shows, the typical workspace is a mix of different kinds of tools. In the variable structure of an information ecology, or how we can designate a scholar's workspace, "[s]imple things are done with simple tools" (Nardi and O'Day, 1999, p. 50). And Orvar Lofgren (2014), another ethnographic observer of scholars at work, finds that many are "euphoric" at first about technology but they discover that "behind the screen is a world of software that organizes knowledge production in subtle and often opaque ways. . . . Software programs create their own routines for searching, storing and retrieving information." The workplace-based studies of the workflow cited in this *Briefing* show that there is more than workflow nostalgia in Lofgren's appreciation of the "sensual dimensions of searching for information, scrolling through files, leafing through volumes in a library, shuffling index cards or following hyperlinks" (p. 81). Thus, becoming a digital scholar happens gradually and many scholars retain analog habits.

THE PATH TO SEAMLESS RESEARCH

What will prompt more confidence in navigating the Internet and capitalizing on new technologies for the workflow? Plainly libraries will have a role, as is argued in a recent report from the Association of Research Libraries

(ARL; Lippincott, 2020). For some scholars, problems of "friction" as John Sack calls them, or the lack of integration among segments of the workflow, can also be addressed with new software. Roger Schonfeld (2018) of Ithaka S+R agrees, seeing greater efficiency and "integrated" or "seamless" research with the adoption of new tools, provided universities are judicious in steering among competing publishers moving quickly to gain an even stronger role in the workflow.

A sociologist told Antonijevic (2015): "I use Dropbox for everything. It has saved my life, it has changed my life" (p. 51). There is testimony in all studies of the workflow about recognition of the affordances of one or another software program, many introduced to the scholarly workflow via libraries. But, surprisingly, there is considerable indifference to well-known programs for citation management, this before they began to incorporate features of social media and before they became units of profit-making journal publishers.

The Cornell group is candid about institutional limits, recognizing individual preferences and the proliferation of software. Thus, according to Nancy Foster (in her "Introduction" to *A Day in the Life*), librarians may be wise not to "urge use of library technologies in the prescribed ways but rather [to accept the] imperfect practices of researchers as reasonable, individual work habits" (Tancheva et al., 2016, p. 10). The report itself adds that "[o]ften the very technology that is meant to make users productive can distract them from focused work" (p. 33). In any case, Antonijevic and Cahoy (2014) report that only about half (sometimes fewer) of the scholars they studied "felt the library should have a role in instructional support relative to the research workflow." Instead, researchers claimed that adopting technology was the "responsibility" of the scholar" (p. 300; see also Koltay, Špiranec, and Karvalics, 2015).

Sack (2017) has a more militant view, "friction is escalating, and piecemeal innovation brings temporary relief only" (p. 22). In effect, scholars are falling behind in adapting to what some information theorists call "Research 2.0" with its new (and constantly newer) digital tools. Tibor Koltay (2015) and his colleagues believe that, like undergraduate students, most researchers are not well prepared to take up the advantages of the new technologies. "It would be utterly naive," they say, "to presume that researchers easily (and readily) accept the need for acquiring information literacy" (p. 88). Scholars and scientists shouldn't assume that they are fully information literate (in the vocabulary of the Association of College and Research Library's ambitious project aimed at students), or in command of Web 2.0, or the expansion of the Internet of early in this century, simply because they are adept at using computers.

DOING THINGS ON THE WEB

Sack (2017) believes that "[o]ur consumer experiences shape our expectations with regard to the possibilities for online work" (p. 21). Scholars will want to be fully active on an integrated platform. "Today's metaphor of the scholarly web is that it is like a library: full of documents to read and to write." But a different metaphor lies ahead:

> Consumers already see the web as a place to *do* things, not just read about them. Even libraries at universities are changing to places where you do things, not just borrow and read documents. The scholarly web will evolve this same way, as workflow goes beyond engagement with the literature and integrates literature into the overall work of the researcher to discover and communicate. (p. 22)

It is just such a view of the role of technology in the workflow that is behind the efforts of FORCE11, the organization advocating the transformation of the workflow with technology. Indeed, the FORCE11 "Manifesto" (https://www.force11.org/about/manifesto) asks about the fate of traditional scholarly tasks: "How can [our] tools be optimally integrated with environments to read, write and edit publications, and to create and evaluate research data?"

Optimism reigns in the introduction of technology into work, particularly in forecasts of the impact of the "second machine age" and its "brilliant technologies," albeit with recognition of what is indispensable in human contributions (e.g., Brynjolfsson and McAfee, 2014). A study of "knowledge workers," presumably inclined to accept help from digitalization, produced a useful graphical representation of how they gained and lost with it (Figure 7.1).

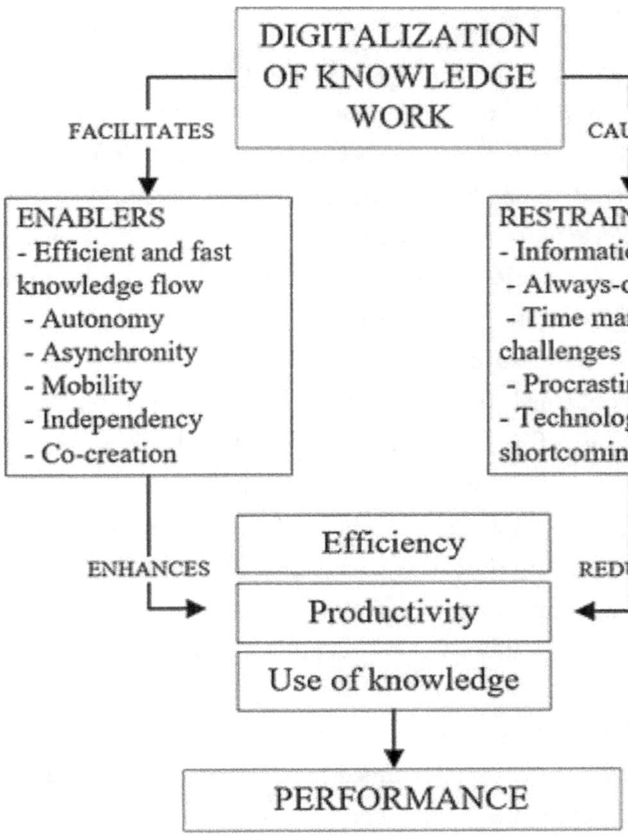

Figure 7.1 Digitalization's Effects on Knowledge Work Performance
Source: Vuori, Helander, and Okkonen (2019)

For Vilma Vuori, Nina Helander, and Jussi Okkonen (2019) the "dream of enhanced performance" is threatened by the realities of technology's actual impact on work. It can "enhance" some features while having the opposite effect on others. Predictably perhaps, the latter category may be more visible in studies of digitalization, as in the feeling of being "always-on" and in complaints about information overload. There is this caution for the workflow: "The more constraints present, the harder it is to realize [the] positive effects" (p. 249).

THE RIGHT BALANCE

Still, at an early and experimental stage in the development of software for the scholarly workflow, there are good reasons to continue to pursue innovations. A step toward easing workflow friction with software is the work done in the final phase (2014–2016) of the Penn State project (Cahoy, 2018). Thus, enhancements were added to Zotero to integrate discovery and self-archiving into the citation management tool. A limited usability study in 2016 with ten participants showed first "continual frustration and unmet desires across multiple phases of the scholarly workflow." But, at least as far as discovery was concerned, scholars were open to embedded services with citation management software. Elyssa Cahoy concluded that if they could manage, as a majority of study participants did, the "high learning barrier for using the "enhanced" software then "the idea of adding on additional services seemed natural and realistic." There remains, however, a "challenge" for libraries "to begin embedding content where our users are rather than where we want them to go (library websites, publisher websites, subscription databases)" (p. 17).

As Cahoy (2018) explains, the evolution of citation management systems in the direction of discovery is aimed at addressing, for researchers, "a desire for better automation across the board" (p. 15). Still, with commercial publishers now having a stake in citation management software, what stance should libraries take toward the consolidation of functions? Bianca Kramer of the University of Utrecht's "101 Innovations" project urges more technology for the workflow but she sees dangers in its commodification:

> It is of course up to any individual researcher to decide whether she/he would want to use [a publisher's suite of workflow apps] in its entirety, but it seems to be to the benefit of the publisher to offer the possibility, and convince institutions to buy into the whole package deal. Such developments would encourage siloing of workflows, with potential limited interoperability with other tools and thus lock into a specific publisher/organization. This is not necessarily a good thing.
>
> (cited in McLemee, 2015; see also Schonfeld, 2018)

Of course, the larger question remains about introducing more technology into the workflow, chiefly for communications via social media. Those who are cautious ask about the role of social media in research itself. David Crotty (2010), now at the Oxford University Press and a blogger (or "chef") at the *Scholarly Kitchen*, said this, no doubt reflecting his PhD training in genetics:

> It's important to remember that the primary job of scientists is doing science, performing experiments, discovering new things. Most social tools for scientists are, by contrast, designed for communication, for talking about science. No matter how great such a tool is, using it is never going to be as important as doing their 'real' work.

Still, Crotty acknowledges what might be ahead. "The best social tools are yet to come," he says, "and they're likely to be directed more toward the actual performance of research."

In considering what is to come, or "emerging technologies," the ARL "mapped" today's landscape in order to identify the most significant categories in which libraries and librarians can be the most effective allies of scholars in their workflow adaptations. They urge finding the right balance in "adopting and experimenting with emerging technologies—the balance between agility and sustainability, convenience and privacy, transformation and persistence" (Lippincott, 2020, p. 16).

CHAPTER 8
SLOWING DOWN IN THE ACCELERATED ACADEMY

The scholarly workflow in the digital age invites a faster pace for research and allied activities, including participation in social media. At the same time, the academic reward system remains rigorous, with high expectations for research productivity. But there are still only twenty-four hours in the day. Perhaps that is why the *Public Library of Science* (PLoS) from the time it was launched in 2003 has claimed to "accelerate the world's research," an especially appealing feature of its megajournal *PLoS ONE* with its thousands of articles published annually. And *arXiv*, the popular preprint server for physics, mathematics, and other quantitative fields, says that the service, presumably now with the many other platforms offering preprints (over sixty according to Johnson and Chiarelli [2019]), is designed to "accelerate the pace of science." Preprints are increasingly recognized as an important feature of the digital evolution of the scholarly communications, their scale reshaping the activity of "dissemination" as it is recognized in workflow schema (Chiarelli et al., 2019).

Indeed there is considerable concern about the impact on work of contemporary experience of time (Taylor, 2014a: Wajcman, 2014). Religious studies scholar Mark Taylor laments that "technologies that were supposed to save time leave us with no time for ourselves" (Taylor, 2014b). And a lesson from sociologist Judith Wajcman's account of the pressures presented by the speed of digital experience is that "We make use of tools, and they return the compliment" (McLemee, 2014), a sentiment well fitted to the "sociomaterial" perspective on work (as in Chapter 1, "From Infrastructure to Ecosystem").

PERILS OF PRODUCTIVITY

Universities, whatever they still represent as enclaves of measured deliberation, in the imagery of the "Ivory Tower," could hardly escape the speeding up of modern life. Indeed, to simplify a complex matter, the managerial transformation of postsecondary education according to neoliberal standards of efficiency, productivity, and market competition, has meant the redefinition of the academic vocations (Bullough, 2014; Cannizzo, 2018). "No Time to Think" is the way scholars, more than a decade ago, began lamenting the conditions of their work (Levy, 2007; Menzies and Newsom, 2007). Since then, a sizeable literature has documented what is now referred to as the "accelerated academy" (as represented in depth by Vostal, 2016; see also Gibbs et al., 2015, and the series on the "Accelerated Academy" at *LSE Blogs*; https://blogs.lse.ac.uk/).

The faculty encounters the accelerated academy in the authority granted to productivity metrics for career advancement and in competitive claims for institutional status and high national and international rankings. A recent study of the research and career paths of sociologists demonstrates how much more is now expected to gain and maintain a place in the field while the time to produce the work remains the same (Warren, 2019). Institutional pressures mean that other disciplines are increasingly organized around encounters with the "accelerated academy." It may surprise professional allies of scholars (like librarians) that there is now research based on a "Publication Pressure Questionnaire," recently revised with attention to "unwanted side effects" (Haven et al., 2019).

Does acceleration mean that in many fields we will see only more work that goes unread and uncited (Baker, 2018)? Still, recognizing the explosion in multiauthored articles (many in science with dozens of authors), there are some who question whether more publishing always means more and thus faster work by individual scholars (Fanelli and Lariviere, 2016).

The danger, of course, in a quickening pace for the research workflow, is failing to make the most of the "brainwork" (as in Chapter 3, "Circuit and Segments") required at each step. The influential critic of the impact of speed on modern culture Robert Hassan (2009) refers to new habits of "abbreviated thinking" in the university. "Computerization is the technological means of speed and neoliberalism its ideological collaborator" (p. 120). If striving for productivity is essential to academic success, then the goal of critical thinking in scholarship can yield to instrumental rationales and methods, and the search for knowledge to focusing on how rapidly data can be made into articles.

BOUNCING, FLICKING, AND SKITTERING

The acceleration of the scholarly workflow is readily visible in recent work on reading (e.g., Durant, 2017). A faster pace for publication may satisfy authors if not readers. For many, more to read means, inevitably, "bouncing," flicking," or "skittering" in encounters with online texts, as Nicholas and Clark (2012) demonstrate in an article in which "Reading" appears in the title in quotation marks (with an implied sneer). Academic readers, they say, "move rapidly along the digital surface, usually with frequent light contacts, or changes of direction. Power browsing has replaced reading" (p. 95), a problem in encounters with texts throughout our culture (Carr, 2010; Love, 2012). Of course, not all scholarly reading is done on screens: more than a third of academic readers print articles and some (8 percent) still read from physical journals (Tenopir, Christian, and Kaufman, 2019).

The UK's Centre for Information Behavior and the Evaluation of Research (CIBER; www.ucl.ac.uk/infostudies/research/ciber/), where David Nicholas and colleagues have been studying scholarly practices for more than a decade, gathered its data on faculty reading via "deep log analysis," sometimes called "digital footprint analysis," based on what is revealed at publishers' servers housing digital versions of thousands of journals. Results show that "the digital transition has resulted in scholars moving from a vertical to a horizontal information seeking and consuming model, a process that leads to them becoming viewers rather than readers" (Nicholas and Clark, 2012, p. 94).

Thus, faculty reading, a key step in the research workflow, has been taking up the style of communications common in the social media, or what is represented by text messaging and Twitter. "In these circumstances long and disciplined reading is becoming a luxury, a thing of the past. Speed is the essence. The only unknown is how fast, abrupt, abbreviated, and cryptic it can really get" (Nicholas and Clark, p. 95). Technology historian and critic Nicholas Carr (2017) has explained "How Smartphones Hijack Our Minds." Such is the academic reading style today that a publisher wondered aloud, in a humorous reference to the business model for journal publishing: "Why not charge for abstracts and give away [full text] PDFs?"

Northwestern University sociologist Gary Fine, a deep reader for decades as the author of many books, is not ready to skip the actual article altogether. But he wants a faster pace for reading, now asking this question: "Is skimming a violation of proper practice, or is it a vital skill that is necessary for occupational success?" He and the graduate students he has been working with in explaining the "active skim" prefer to think of it as "legitimate deviance" according to the norms of academic and intellectual life, and the choices to be made about the workflow for particular research projects. Thus, "[r]eading is not a single activity, but rather it is a set of practices that depend on the form and style of the text and on goals, intentions, and demands placed on the reader." And there is this lexical sleight of hand, in effect a reflection on all elements of the digital scholarly workflow: "In most fields—perhaps in all—it is hard to imagine a successful or admired student who has not learned how to read without slow care. Skimming is, or should be, fast care" (Wohl and Fine, 2017, pp. 226–27).

If scholarly reading is now focused on fragments of content, purposeful uses are made of it. There has been a change in the scholarly workflow, where once information seeking was simply the first step in discovery it is now done continuously. Fine and his students advocate "learning how not to read or . . . to read certain texts incompletely." They suggest techniques for the productive "active skim" featuring attention to only parts of texts. A successful "active skimmer" is quoted with the advice she gives (with Fine's apparent support) to other graduate students: "The first thing I tell [them] is that 'your job is not to read—your job is to extract information'." Many scholars, if perhaps reflecting what Nicholas and Clark refer to as a "nostalgic ideal," would say that the "active skim" is a troubling definition of the goals of reading, at least of texts written to present serious ideas and complex human experiences.

Other parts of the workflow might also benefit from slowing down, with the "deliberate subversion of time" yielding more learning (Harland, 2016). Tibor Koltay (2017) urges "slow search." True enough, Internet search is supposed to be fast. But patience can offer the reward of the most pertinent and suggestive resources. In fact, Koltay favors the larger category of "slow principles" for research and scholarly communications. The key is gaining control of resources according to what they remand for understanding:

> Following slow principles is not identical with doing something less rapidly. It is rather being concerned with control by judging the right speed and tempo for a given activity and the context, with a reflective attitude that is basically identical with the ideals that manifest in information literacy's critical stance.

Koltay acknowledges the pressures to "consume and produce" knowledge but he urges the adoption of slow principles "appropriate to a given situation" (p. 771). There are no rules for putting your foot on the brakes but scholars should be alert to activities in the workflow where slowing the pace can be fruitful.

CHANGING GEARS

As perception of the acceleration of academic life has gained ground, protests have featured the need to protect faculty time (e.g., Gill, 2009). In *The Slow Professor*, Maggie Berg and Barbra Seeber (2016) invoke the maxim of environmentalist David Orr (2002), a reminder of the framework for thinking about the workflow with which this *Briefing* began: "Fast knowledge is mostly linear; slow knowledge is complex and ecological" (cited in Berg and Seeber, 2016, p. 58). They celebrate the "slow professor" as a challenge to the neoliberal managerial style that prizes efficiency and productivity, a target of considerable critical writing on higher education (e.g., Cannizzo, 2018; Hassan, 2017). But for Berg and Seeber "slow" does not mean inefficient or unproductive in encountering the accelerated academy.

> Slowing down is about asserting the importance of contemplation, connectedness, fruition, and complexity. It gives meaning to letting research take the

> time it needs to ripen and makes it easier to resist the pressure to be faster. It gives meaning to thinking about scholarship as a community, not a competition. It gives meaning to periods of rest, an understanding that research does not run like a mechanism; there are rhythms, which include pauses and periods that may seem unproductive.
>
> (p. 57)

Berg and Seeber borrow from the ideology of the "Slow Movement" and its critique of market-based standards for everyday living.

What professor doesn't wish for complete autonomy in setting the pace of academic work? The image of the neoliberal university has prompted contempt for it among professors who may know little about it beyond its role as a common epithet in the critical literature on higher education. But there is the feeling of being unduly burdened with institutional chores while expectations for grants and publishing increase. And performance "measures" feature only what can be counted, from citations to visibility—registered by altmetrics—in social media. The danger, of course, is in acceleration of the workflow to keep up with institutional expectations, or even, reflecting the pursuit of reputation, a "selling-out" of academic values (Gruber, 2014). British scholar Stephen Ball (2003) asks these compelling questions about our scholarly routines: "Are we doing this because it is important, because we believe in it, because it is worthwhile? Or is it being done ultimately because it will be measured or compared?" (cited in Harland, 2016, p. 179).

Still, a leading scholar of acceleration warns about the risks of underestimating how speed can be a legitimate and fruitful feature of academic work. Filip Vostal (2016) accepts the perception of contemporary academic experience as accelerated but cautions about representing "slow" as a "lifestyle choice" from within a secure foundation of professional employment, and unavailable to the increasing numbers of part-time or contingent postsecondary teachers. He objects (in Carrigan and Vostal, 2016) to an "incorrect impression that academia is flooded with stress, despair, and misery." Thus, the scholarly workflow is a highly variable part of academic vocations:

> Whether one is distracted, accelerated, stressed, burned out or just about the opposite—whether one thrives and enjoys plenty of quality and unhasty time—very much depends on . . . relevant variables such as age, gender, academic status, discipline, family situation, [and] psychological disposition.

Also, those who see only the "fast lane" in the scholarly workflow may ignore positive attributes of "enabling acceleration" distinct from those associated with the neoliberal "business model" of the university.

Vostal (2016) has no wish to underestimate negative consequences of a faster pace prompted by institutional policies, but for research and other academic activities he suggests the operational principle of "slow when needed and fast when convenient" (p. 198). He might have added appealing. One of his interview subjects said, "For me the key part of being an academic is to be able to keep up with the [fast] information flow. . . . because this is essentially what being an academic is" (p. 130). A chemist recalled for Vostal what it took to locate and get a copy of a journal article until IT accelerated this part of the workflow: "Now I can just click, get the article and it is right here, [and] I am reading it" (p. 129). And a historian said: "It is always nice to be in the fifth gear for a while but then to be in the first or second. I like being able to change gears" (pp. 125–26). In other words, the scholarly workflow is pliable. As Vostal puts it: "Acceleration may be negotiated and does not necessarily determine or eliminate temporal autonomy" (p. 117). Scholars can capitalize on their "subjective subtlety and temporal resourcefulness" in finding a satisfying pace for their work (see also Vostal, 2019).

CONCLUSION

THE EVOLVING WORKFLOW AND THE DIGITAL SCHOLAR

This *Briefing* has featured the constellation of activities, old and new, associated with the scholarly workflow. It extends now into fast and far-reaching communications and supports novel forms of academic craftsmanship. David Weinberger's celebration of the digital conditions of our lives and work—in *Everyday Chaos: Technology, Complexity, and How We're Thriving in a New World of Possibility* (2019)—also reflects the well-known uneasiness in our society about the forces shaping our thoughts and actions. Scholars' stake in the digital age is operational, in the electronic workflow, professional, in estimating the nature and future of networked academic careers, and perhaps even philosophical, in appraising the meanings of far-reaching change. Who isn't a digital scholar, whether zealous or cautious about innovation in academic work?

According to Marshall McLuhan, time is the essential element of context in thinking about the influence of technology. In 1962, he began *The Gutenberg Galaxy* on a reassuring note: "We are today as far into the electric age as the Elizabethans had advanced into the typographical and mechanical age. And we are experiencing the same confusions and indecisions which they had felt when living simultaneously in two contrasted forms of society and experience" (p. 1). James Gleick (2011) cites McLuhan but with uncertainty about whether having been there before, as is often said about the strain of information overload, will be the foundation for only another demanding period of adaptation. Thus, with the vast scale of change in this century and the extent of digital connectedness, Gleick corrects McLuhan: "As much as it is the same, this time it is different." He acknowledges our ambivalence about technology's effects: "We veer from elation to dismay and back" (p. 413). Now, in a time of dismay deepened by the COVID-19 pandemic of 2020, we can wonder about the durability of its effects on scholarly and scientific habits. An early estimate names financial vulnerability in higher education and then, of course, for academic libraries and university presses, a priority for digital first communications, a decline in travel and thus conferences and other traditional forms of professional interaction (Michael et al., 2020).

Attention to the scholarly workflow, as this *Briefing* is designed to show, prompts a divided view of whether the digital age is truly unique. There is no question of the advantages that have come to scholarly inquiry from the latest technology. But there is awareness too of new problems scholars share with everyone working largely online, including the impact of reading on screens and what it prompts in unwelcome cognitive change (Wolf, 2018). And there is allied uneasiness about the uses of social media, particularly when their communicative benefits are weighed against what they present in distractions (e.g., Newport, 2019). However much the scholarly workflow reflects zeal for technological innovation, scrutiny of its impact on reading and communications will, ideally, make scholars diligent students of the digital age while they labor in it.

While the scholarly workflow is changing to reflect digital opportunities, as in formulations of the "Digital Scholar" (Lupton, Mewburn, and Thomson, 2018; Weller, 2018) or "Research 2.0" (Koltay, Špiranic, and Karvalics, 2015), it is doing so only according to habits and preferences that remain part of the research vocations and in the context of turmoil in the publishing system. "Getting the whole picture is quite difficult since new tools continuously emerge and evolve through interactions with other tools" (Orlandi et al., 2019, p. 59). Still, there is a difference between the state of the art and (so to speak) the state of the actual, or the gap between what is anticipated by digital innovators and what claims the attention of most scholars, including those who have grown up with technology.

The vanguard in scholarly communications is eager for us to engage with artificial intelligence (AI) as it expands its role throughout society. Thus, John Sack (2017) looks forward to the benefits of "precision scholarship" made possible by machine reading. Its place in the workflow would be "knowing which topics you are personally interested in and finding the relevant texts and data, [and] presenting them with annotations and highlights." Indeed, "reading" understates what such technology would do. "The machine will not only read the literature, but it will *write* the literature that you, specifically, must know about." And such machine learning is not so far away: "It is hard to imagine it taking any longer than, say, autonomous automobiles" (p. 22).

We know now that recent predictions that such vehicles were only a few years away have been undermined by a dose of realism about the pace of innovation and the preferences of drivers and pedestrians (Boudette, 2019). A 2019 roundtable on AI organized by the *Scholarly Kitchen* (Michael, 2019) recognized the urgency of AI in considerations of scholarly communications. One participant claimed that AI "has the ability to push academia to the next level." But another, while recognizing what AI might contribute to scholarship, offered this reminder about the human dynamics of the workflow: "The great intellectual leaps that generate whole new avenues of research may never come from a machine" (see also Webb, 2019).

The arrival of the fully capable digital scholar, prepared to revise all research conventions, and perhaps even accept AI in the workflow, will take time. True enough, there is wide acceptance of digitalization in search, storage, and communications. But the core of the workflow, with its focus on producing frequent publications in high-status journals, remains (Harley, 2013). Indeed, as noted in Chapter 8, a study of academic careers in sociology showed that publishing expectations for those seeking first jobs and then promotion to tenure had doubled in recent decades (Warren, 2019). The situation is similar in virtually all disciplines: publishing rules in the academic reward system as fiercely as ever. Thus, it is hardly a surprise that an ambitious three-year study (2016–2018) of early career researchers in seven countries showed almost all, however much they have adapted their workflows to the digital age, particularly in collaborating and in communicating with social media, are preoccupied with publishing, citation metrics, and reputation (Nicholas et al., 2019). Whatever postsecondary educational reformers may wish for in more attention to teaching and service, the assessment system, with what it encourages in accelerated performance, appears everywhere to be set in stone.

Even so, there are features of the digital transformation being welcomed. There is no question, as all studies show, that scholars and scientists are making extensive use of online journals and of Google Scholar. That much is clear from ITHAKA S+R's latest faculty survey (Blankstein and Wolff-Eisenberg, 2019). Like the studies of early career scholars, it confirms the commitment of most American scholars and scientists to the traditional scholarly communications system with its academic rewards. In effect, it demonstrates that while there is considerable change underway in the digital workflow, it is within the context of practices reflecting well-established professional routines. ITHAKA S+R's ongoing series of studies of "changing research practices" across the disciplines presents a mixed picture of scholarly uses of technology, with some scholars in some fields gaining expertise in new tools and methods while others lag behind in capitalizing on them and on technologically oriented services offered by academic libraries. Prospects are uncertain for the transformation of the workflow as a joint project of disciplines and libraries. Speaking of how important it is to manage the workflow according to individual needs, one respondent told an ITHAKA S+R researcher that "each scholar in [their] field is kind of a mini-librarian" (Cooper, 2018, p. 21).

The scholarly foundation for academic careers may be stronger than ever but the scholarly workflow is evolving, reflecting both the availability of new digital resources and the choices individual scholars make in their practices at different rates and with different expectations for research innovations. In a well-functioning "information ecology," new technologies "are carefully integrated into existing habits and practices" (Nardi and O'Day, 1999, p. 50). The ecological process of "integration," mediating at different rates between many forces, can itself yield fruitful and lasting results. It is often observed that postsecondary institutions are slow to change (Tagg, 2012). Historian of higher education David Labaree (2017) believes that the competing interests in the system making this so—amounting to a "perfect mess"—are actually its strength.

The scholarly workflow presents habits and opportunities. Critics of its conventions bemoan "fragmentation" and hope for a more fully realized digital future. The evolving workflow, rather than one transformed by the digital age, allows for change at a pace that suits individual professional preferences in an ecology of scholarly communications supporting countless configurations of methods and tools, old and new. Productive scholars, welcoming some innovations but indifferent to others, and mindful of what is needed for a successful academic career, can agree with what one told an interviewer about how he manages his scholarly workflow, including what may be added to his identity as a digital scholar: "I do what works for me" (Kaye et al., 2006, p. 277).

WORKS CITED

Abbott, A. (2014). *Digital Paper: A Manual for Research and Writing with Library and Internet Materials*. Chicago, IL: University of Chicago Press.

Abrahamson, E., & Freedman, D. (2007). *A Perfect Mess: The Hidden Benefits of Disorder*. New York: Little Brown.

Acord, S., & Harley, D. (2013). Credit, Time, and Personality: The Human Challenges to Sharing Scholarly Work Using Web 2.0. *New Media & Society*, *15*(3), 379–397.

American Council of Learned Societies. (2006). *Our Cultural Commonwealth: The Report of the American Council of Learned Societies on Cyberinfrastructure for the Humanities and Social Sciences*. New York: ACLS.

Annual Reviews. (2011). *The Role of the Critical Review Article in Alleviating Information Overload*. Palo Alto, CA: Annual Reviews.

Antonijevic, S. (2015). *Amongst Digital Humanists: An Ethnographic Study of Digital Knowledge Production*. New York: Palgrave Macmillan.

Antonijevic, S., & Cahoy, A. (2014). Personal Library Curation: An Ethnographic Study of Scholars' Information Practices. *portal: Libraries and the Academy*, *14*(2), 287–306.

Antonijevic, S., & Cahoy, E. S. (2018). Researcher as Bricoleur: Contextualizing Humanists' Digital Workflows. *DHQ: Digital Humanities Quarterly*, *12*(3).

Baker, S. (2018). How Much Research Goes Completely Uncited? *Times Higher Education*, April 18.

Ball, S. J. (2003). The Teacher's Soul and the Terrors of Performativity. *Journal of Education Policy*, *18*(2), 215–228.

Bawden, D., & Robinson, L. (2009). The Dark Side of Information: Overload, Anxiety, and Other Paradoxes and Pathologies. *Journal of Information Science*, *35*(2), 180–191.

Bawden, D., & Robinson, L. (2020). Information Overload: An Overview. In D. Redlawsk (Ed.), *Oxford Encyclopedia of Political Decision Making*. Oxford, UK: Oxford University Press.

Bell, D. (2005). The Bookless Future: What the Internet Is Doing to Scholarship. *The New Republic*, May 2, 27–30.

Berg, M., & Seeber, B. (2016). *The Slow Professor: Challenging the Culture of Speed in the Academy*. Toronto: University of Toronto Press.

Blair, A. (2011). *Too Much to Know: Managing Scholarly Information before the Modern Age.* New Haven, CT: Yale University Press.

Blankstein, M., & Wolff-Eisenberg, C. (2019). *ITHAKA S+R US Faculty Survey 2018.* New York: ITHAKA S+R.

Blummer, B., & Kenton, J. M. (2018). A Systematic Review of E-Books in Academic Libraries: Access, Advantages, and Usage. *New Review of Academic Librarianship, 23*(4), 1–28.

Booth, C. (2011). Reflective Teaching, Effective Learning: Instructional Resources for Library Educators. Chicago, IL: American Library Association.

Borgman, C. (2007). *Scholarship in the Digital Age: Information, Infrastructure, and the Internet.* Cambridge, MA: MIT Press.

Bosman, J., & Kramer, B. (2015). 101 Innovations in Scholarly Communications. LSE Impact Blog, November 11.

Boudette, N. (2019). Despite High Hopes, Self-Driving Cars Are "Way in the Future." *New York Times*, July 17.

Brynjolfsson, E., & McAfee, A. (2014). *The Second Machine Age: Work, Progress, and Prosperity in a Time of Brilliant Technologies.* New York: Norton.

Bullough, R. (2014, Fall/Winter). Higher Education and the Neoliberal Threat: Place, Fast Time, and Identity. *Journal of Thought, 49*, 13–32.

Bussert, K., Chiang, K., & Tancheva, K. (2011). Personal Management of Scholarly Information. In N. Foster, K. Clark, K. Tancheva, & R. Kilzer (Eds.), *Scholarly Practice, Participatory Design and the Extensible Catalog* (pp. 123–150). Chicago, IL: Association of College and Research Libraries.

Cahoy, E. (2013). Faculty Members as Archivists: Personal Archiving Practices in the Academic Environment. In D. Hawkins (Ed.), *Personal Archiving: Preserving our Digital Heritage* (pp. 137–152). Medford, NJ: Information Today.

Cahoy, E. (2018). Leave the Browser Behind: Placing Discovery within the User's Workflow. *Liber Quarterly, 28*(1), 1–19.

Cannizzo, F. (2018). Tactical Evaluations: Everyday Neoliberalism in Academia. *Journal of Sociology, 54*(1), 1–15.

Carr, N. (2010). *The Shallows: What the Internet Is Doing to Our Brains.* New York: Norton.

Carr, N. (2017). How Smartphones Highjack Our Minds. *Wall Street Journal*, October 6.

Carrigan, M., & Vostal, F. (2016). Not So Fast! A Critique of the "Slow Professor." *University Affairs*, April 22.

Chiarelli, A., Johnson, R., Pinfield, S., & Richens, E. (2019). Preprints and Scholarly Communications: An Exploratory Qualitative Study of Adoption, Practices, Drivers and Barriers. *F1000Research, 8*, 971.

Cloutier, C. (2016). How I Write: An Inquiry Into the Writing Practices of Academics. *Journal of Management Inquiry, 25*(1), 69–84.

Cooper, D. (2018). *Supporting the Research Practices of Asian Studies Scholars.* New York: ITHAKA S+R.

Courtright, C. (2007). Context in Information Behavior. *Annual Review of Information Science and Technology, 41*, 273–306.

Crotty, D. (2010). Science and Web 2.0: Talking Science vs. Doing Science. *Scholarly Kitchen*, February 8.

Duffy, B., & Pooley, J. (2017). "Facebook for Academics": The Convergence of Self-Branding and Social Media Logic on Academia.edu. *Social Media + Society*, January–March: 1–11.

Durant, D. (2017). *Reading in a Digital Age*. Charleston, SC: ATG Media.

Elder Jr., G. H., & Rockwell, R. C. (1979). The Life-Course and Human Development: An Ecological Perspective. *International Journal of Behavioral Development, 2*(1), 1–21.

Eldermire, E., & Tang, N. (2016). So Everyday: Interviews with Academic Researchers to Understand Their Day-to-Day. In *Proceedings of the 2016 Library Assessment Conference* (pp. 414–418). Washington, DC: Association of Research Libraries.

Evans, J. (2008). Electronic Publication and the Narrowing of Science and Scholarship. *Science 321*(5887), 395–399.

Falciani-White, N. (2016). Understanding the "Complexity of Experience": Modeling Faculty Research Practices. *Journal of Academic Librarianship, 42*(2), 118–126.

Falciani-White, N. (2017). Information Behaviors of Elite Scholars in the Context of Academic Practice. *Journal of Documentation, 73*(5), 953–973.

Fanelli, D., & Laviriere, V. (2016). Researchers' Publication Rate Has Not Increased in a Century. *PLoS One, 11*(3), e0149504.

Gessner, G., Eldermire, E., Tang, N., & Tancheva, K. (2017). The Research Lifecycle and the Future of Research Libraries: A Library of Apps. *Proceedings of 2017 Conference of the Association of College and Research Libraries*, pp. 533–543.

Gibbs, P., Ylijoki, O., Guzmán-Valenzuela, C., & Barnett, R. (Eds.). (2015). *Universities in the Flux of Time: An Exploration of Time and Temporality in University Life*. New York: Routledge.

Gibney, E. (2014). How to Tame the Flood of Literature. *Nature, 513*, 129–130.

Gill, R. (2009). Breaking the Silence: The Hidden Injuries of Neo-Liberal Academia. In R. Flood & R. Gill (Eds.), *Secrecy and Silence in the Research Process: Feminist Reflections* (pp. 228–244). London: Routledge

Gleick, J. (2011). *The Information: A History, a Theory, a Flood*. New York: Pantheon.

Golden, T. (2011). Too Much to Know. *Inside Higher Ed*, March 17.

Gruber, T. (2014). Academic Sell-Out: How an Obsession with Metrics and Rankings Is Damaging Academia. *Journal of Marketing for Higher Education, 24*(2), 165–177.

Gusenbauer, M. (2019). Google Scholar to Overshadow Them All? Comparing the Sizes of 12 Academic Search Engines and Bibliographic Satabases. *Scientometrics, 118*(1), 177–214.

Harland, T. (2016). Deliberate Subversion of Time: Slow Scholarship and Learning through research. In F. Trede & C. McEwen (Eds.), *Educating the Deliberate Professional* (pp. 175–-188). Cham, CH: Springer International.

Harley, D. (2013). Scholarly Communication: Cultural Contexts, Evolving Models. *Science, 342*(6154), 80–82.

Hassan, R. (2009). *Empires of Speed: Time and the Acceleration of Politics and Society*. Boston, MA: Brill.

Hassan, R. (2017). The Worldly Space: The Digital University in Networked Time. *British Journal of Sociology of Education, 38*(1), 72–82.

Haven, T., de Goede, M., Tijdink, J., & Oort, F. (2019). Personally Perceived Publication Pressure: Revising the Publication Pressure Questionnaire by Using Work Stress Models. *Research Integrity and Peer Review, 4*, 7.

Hillesund, T. (2010). Digital Reading Spaces: How Expert Readers Handle Books, the Web and Electronic Paper. *First Monday*, April.

Johnson, C. (2012). Bricoleur and Bricolage: From Metaphor to Universal Concept. *Paragraph, 35*(3), 355–372.

Johnson, R., & Chiarelli, A. (2019). The Second Wave of Preprint Servers: How Can Publishers Keep Afloat? *Scholarly Kitchen*, October 16.

Jones, W. (2007). *Keeping Found Things Found: The Study and Practice of Personal Information Management.* Burlington, MA: Morgan Kaufman.

Kaye, J., Vertesi, J., Avery, S., Dafoe, A., David, S., Onaga, L., Rosero, I, & Pinch, T. (2006). To Have and to Hold: Exploring the Personal Archive. In *Proceedings of the ACM SIGCHI Conference on Human Factors in Computing Systems (CHI 2006)* (pp. 275–284). New York: ACM.

Kim, Y., & Zhong, C. (2017). Ideas Rise from Chaos: Information Structure and Creativity. *Organizational Behavior and Human Decision Processes, 138*, 15–27.

Koltay, T. (2017). The Bright Side of Information: Ways of Mitigating Information Overload. *Journal of Documentation, 73*(4), 767–775.

Koltay, T., Špiranec, S., & Karvalics, L. Z. (2015). The Shift of Information Literacy towards Research 2.0. *Journal of Academic Librarianship, 41*(1), 87–93.

Labaree, D. (2017). *A Perfect Mess: The Unlikely Ascendancy of American Higher Education.* Chicago, IL: University of Chicago Press.

Lambotte, F., & Meunier, D. (2013). From Bricolage to Thickness: Making the Most of the Messiness of Research Narratives. *Qualitative Research in Organizations and Management, 8*(1), 85–100.

Levitin, D. (2014). *The Organized Mind: Thinking Straight in the Age of Information Overload.* New York: Dutton.

Levy, D. (2007). No Time to Think: Reflections on Information Technology and Contemplative Scholarship. *Ethics and Information Technology, 9*(4), 237–249.

Lippincott, S. (2020). *Mapping the Current Landscape of Research Library Engagement With Emerging Technologies in Research and Learning.* Edited by Mary Lee Kennedy, Clifford Lynch, and Scout Calvert. Washington, DC: Association of Research Libraries, Hadley, MA: Born-Digital, Washington, DC: Coalition for Networked Information, and Washington, DC: EDUCAUSE.

Lofgren, O. (2014). Routinising Research: Academic Skills in Analogue and Digital Worlds. *International Journal of Social Research Methodology, 17*(1), 73–86.

Love, J. (2012). Reading Fast and Slow. *The American Scholar, 81*(2), 64–72.

Lupton, D., Mewburn, I., & Thomson, P. (2018). *The Digital Academic: Critical Perspectives on Digital Technologies in Higher Education.* New York: Routledge.

Makri, S., & Blandford, A. (2012). Coming across Information Serendipitously—Part 1: A Process Model. *Journal of Documentation, 68*(5), 684–705.

Marshall, C. (2008). From Writing and Analysis to the Repository: Taking the Scholars' Perspective on Scholarly Archiving. In *Proceedings of the 8th ACM/IEEE-CS Joint Conference on Digital Libraries*, June, pp. 251–260.

McKay, D., Chang, S., Smith, W., & Buchanan, G. (2019). The Things We Talk about When We Talk about Browsing: An Empirical Typology of Library Browsing Behavior. *Journal of the Association for Information Science and Technology, 70*(12), 1383–1394.

McLemee, S. (2014). Pressed for Time. *Inside Higher Ed*, November 5.

McLemee, S. (2015). The Shape of Things to Come. *Inside Higher Ed*, January 28.

McLuhan, M. (1962). *The Gutenberg Galaxy: The Making of Typographic Man.* Toronto: University of Toronto Press.

Menzies, H., & Newson, J. (2007). No Time to Think: Academics' Life in the Globally Wired University. *Time and Society, 16*(1), 83–98.

Meyer, E., & Schroeder, R. (2009). The World Wide Web of Research and Access to Knowledge. *Knowledge Management Research and Practice, 7*, 218–233.

Michael, A. (2019). Ask the Chefs: AI and Scholarly Communications. *Scholarly Kitchen*, April 25.

Michael, A., Anderson, R., Meadows, A., Wulf, K., Smith, D., Vines, T., Mudditt, A., & Luther, J. (2020). Ask the Chefs: Permanent Change? *Scholarly Kitchen*, May 28.

Monroe-Gulick, A., Valentine, G., & Brocks-Kieffer, J. (2017). "You Need to Have the Street Beat": A Qualitative Study of Faculty Research Needs and Challenges. *portal: Libraries and the Academy, 17*(4), 777–802.

Moore, M., & Singley, E. (2019). Understanding the Information Behaviors of Doctoral Students: An Exploratory Study. *portal: Libraries and the Academy, 19*(2), 279–293.

Nardi, B., & O'Day, V. (1999). *Information Ecologies: Using Technology with Heart.* Cambridge, MA: MIT Press.

National Science Foundation. (2003). *Revolutionizing Science and Engineering through Cyberinfrastructure.* Washington, DC: NSF.

Nentwich, M., &Koenig, R. (2014). Academia Goes Facebook? The Potential of Social Network Sites in the Scholarly Realm. In S. Barling & S. Friesike (Eds.), *Opening Science: The Evolving Guide on How the Internet is Changing Research, Collaboration, and Scholarly Publishing* (pp. 107–124). Cham, Germany: SpringerOpen.

Newman, M., & Sack, J. (2013). Information Workflow of Academic Researchers in the Evolving Information Environment: An Interview Study. *Learned Publishing, 26*(2), 123–131.

Newport, C. (2019). *Digital Minimalism: Choosing a Focused Way of Life in a Noisy World.* New York: Portfolio.

Nicholas, D., & Clark, D. (2012). "Reading" in the Digital Environment. *Learned Publishing, 25*(2), 93–98.

Nicholas, D., & Clark, D. (2015). Finding Stuff. In M. Moss & B. Endicott-Popovsky (Eds.), *Is Digital Different?: How Information Creation, Capture, Preservation and Discovery Are Being Transformed* (pp. 19–34). London: Facet.

Nicholas, D., Watkinson, A., Boukacem-Zeghmouri, C., Rodriguez-Bravo, B., Xu, J., Abrizah, A., Świgoń, M., Clark, D., & Hermman, E. (2019). So, Are Early Career Researchers the Harbingers of Change? *Learned Publishing, 32*, 237–247.

Orlandi, L., Ricciardi, F., Rossignoli, C., and De Marco, M. (2019). Scholarly Work in the Internet Age: Co-evolving Technologies, Institutions and Workflows. *Journal of Innovation & Knowledge, 4*(1), 55–61.

Orlikowski, W. (2007). Sociomaterial Practices: Exploring Technology at Work. *Organization Studies, 28*(9), 1435–1448.

Orlikowski, W. (2010). The Sociomateriality of Organizational Life: Considering Technology in Management Research. *Cambridge Journal of Economics, 34*, 125–141.

Orr, D. (2002). *The Nature of Design: Ecology, Culture, and Human Intention.* Oxford: Oxford University Press.

Palmer, C., Teffeau, L., & Pirmann, C. (2009). *Scholarly Information Practices in the Online Environment: Themes from the Literature and Implications for Library Service Development.* Dublin, OH: Online Computer Library Center.

Sack, J. (2017). Friction in the Scholarly Workflow: Obstacles and Opportunities. *Information Services and Use, 37,* 17–22.

Schonfeld, R. (2018). *Big Deal: Should Universities Outsource More Core Research Infrastructure?* New York: ITHAKA S+R.

Snow, C. (1959). *The Two Cultures and the Scientific Revolution.* Cambridge: Cambridge University Press.

Tagg, J. (2012). Why Does the Faculty Resist Change? *Change, 44*(1), 6–15.

Tancheva, C., Gessner, G., Tang, N., Eldermire, E., Furnas, H., Branchini, D., & Steinhart, G. (2016). *A Day in the Life of a (Serious) Researcher: Envisioning the Future of the Research Library.* New York: ITHAKA S+R.

Taylor, M. (2014a). *Speed Limits: Where Time Went and Why We Have So Little Left.* New Haven, CT: Yale University Press.

Taylor, M. (2014b). Speed Kills: Fast Is Never Enough. *Chronicle of Higher Education,* October 20.

Tenopir C., Christian L., & Kaufman J. (2019). Seeking, Reading, and Use of Scholarly Articles: An International Study of Perceptions and Behavior of Researchers. *Publications, 7*(1), 18.

Ulibarri, N., Cravens, A., Nabergoj, A., Kernbach, S., & Royalty, A. (2019). *Creativity in Research: Cultivate Clarity, Be Innovative, and Make Progress in Your Research Journey.* Cambridge, UK: Cambridge University Press.

Unsworth, J. (2000). Scholarly Primitives: What Methods Do Humanities Researchers Have in Common, and How Might Our Tools Reflect This? In *Symposium on Humanities Computing: Formal Methods, Experimental Practice. King's College, London,* vol. 13, May 13.

Van Noorden, R. (2014). Google Scholar Pioneer on Search Engine's Future. *Nature,* November 7.

Vohs, K. (2013). It's Not "Mess." It's Creativity. *New York Times,* September 13.

Vohs, K., Redden, J., & Rahinel, R. (2014). Physical Order Produces Healthy Choices, Generosity, Conventionality, Whereas Disorder Produces Creativity. *Psychological Science, 24*(9), 1860–1867.

Vostal, F. (2016). *Accelerating Academia: The Changing Structure of Academic Time.* New York: Palgrave Macmillan.

Vostal, F. (2019). Slowing Down Modernity: A Critique. *Time and Society, 28*(3), 1039–60.

Vuori, V., Helander, N., & Okkonen, J. (2019). Digitalization in Knowledge Work: The Dream of Enhanced Performance. *Cognition, Technology, and* Work, 21, 237–252.

Wajcman, J. (2014). *Pressed for Time: The Acceleration of Life in Digital Capitalism.* Chicago, IL: University of Chicago Press.

Warren, J. (2019). How Much Do You Have to Publish to Get a Job in a Top Sociology Department? Or to Get Tenure? Trends over a Generation. *Sociological Science, 6,* 172–96.

Webb, A. (2019). *The Big Nine: How the Tech Titans and Their Thinking Machines Could Warp Humanity.* New York: Public Affairs.

Weinberger, D. (2019). *Everyday Chaos: Technology, Complexity, and How We're Thriving in a New World of Possibility.* Cambridge, MA: Harvard Business Review Press.

Weller, M. (2018). The Digital Scholar Revisited. *Philosopher's Lab, 1*(2), 52–71.

Wellmon, C. (2015). *Organizing Enlightenment: Information Overload and the Invention of the Modern Research University*. Baltimore, MD: Johns Hopkins University Press.

Wellmon, C. (2016, Summer). The Future of Search. *Hedgehog Review*, *18*(2), 116–119.

Wohl, H., & Fine, G. (2017). The Active Skim: Efficient Reading as a Moral Challenge in Postgraduate Education. *Teaching Sociology*, *45*(3), 220–227.

Wolf, M. (2018). *Reader, Come Home: The Reading Brain in a Digital World*. New York: HarperCollins.

Yaqub, O. (2018). Serendipity: Towards a Taxonomy and a Theory. *Research Policy*, *47*, 169–179.

Yoe, M. (2001). Kings of Chaos. *University of Chicago Magazine*, June.

ABOUT THE AUTHOR

Steven Weiland is a Professor in the Graduate Program in Higher Education at Michigan State University where he teaches courses in adult career development, education in the digital age, and scholarly communications. He is the author of *Intellectual Craftsmen: Ways and Works in American Scholarship* and co-editor of *Jazz in Mind: Essays on the History and Meanings of Jazz.*

www.ingramcontent.com/pod-product-compliance
Lightning Source LLC
LaVergne TN
LVHW062318240826
846302LV00006B/21
9781941269442